CULTURES OF THE WORLD®

MOZAMBIQUE

David C. King

 **Marshall Cavendish** Benchmark
New York

PICTURE CREDITS

Cover photo: © Sean Sprague/The Image Works
AFP: 94 • age fotostock/SEAN SPRAGUE: 71 • alt.TYPE/Reuters: 11, 15, 31, 35, 36, 38, 41, 45, 52, 54, 60, 61, 62, 64, 65, 76, 119 • Andrew Bannister/South Photographs/africanpictures.net: 120 • Audrius Tomonis: 135 • Bes Stock: 3, 5, 17, 34, 81, 82, 83, 86, 90, 91, 95, 96, 97, 102, 118, 128, 129, 130, 131 • David Larsen/The Media Bank/africanpictures.net: 16, 55 • Eye Ubiquitous/Gary Trotter: 109 • Getty Images: 12, 40, 48, 59, 111 • Guy Stubbs/Independent Contributors/africanpictures. net: 106, 123, 125 • ImageHub: 70, 84, 85, 126 • IMAGES24.co.za/Dook: 72 • Jason Laure: 8, 9, 10, 14, 20, 22, 24, 28, 49, 51, 68, 69, 73, 74, 75, 78, 79, 100, 101, 103, 104, 107, 108, 110, 117 • John Robinson/South Photographs/africanpictures.net: 6 • Linda Martindale/africanpictures.net: 1, 63 • Lori Waselchuk/South Photographs/africanpictures.net: 93 • PhotographersDirect.com: 87, 88, 122, 124 • Richard Wareham/Sylvia Cordaiy Photo Library: 7, 13 • Tropix: 4, 18, 19, 42, 47, 50, 53, 58, 112, 115, 89

PRECEDING PAGE
Two Mozambican teenagers smile for the camera.

Marshall Cavendish Benchmark
99 White Plains Road
Tarrytown, NY 10591
Website: www.marshallcavendish.us

© Marshall Cavendish International (Asia) Private Limited 2006
® "Cultures of the World" is a registered trademark of Marshall Cavendish Corporation.

Series concept and design by Times Editions
An imprint of Marshall Cavendish International (Asia) Private Limited
A member of Times Publishing Limited

Library of Congress Cataloging-in-Publication Data
King, David C.
   Mozambique / by David C. King.—1st ed.
      p. cm.—(Cultures of the world)
   Summary: "Provides comprehensive information on the geography, history, governmental
      structure, economy, cultural diversity, peoples, religion, and culture of Mozambique—Provided
      by publisher.
   Includes bibliographical references and index.
   ISBN-13: 978-0-7614-2331-7
   ISBN-10: 0-7614-2331-1
   1. Mozambique—Juvenile literature. I. Title. II. Cultures of the World
   DT3299.K56 2007
   967.9—dc22   2006002302

Printed in China

7 6 5 4 3 2 1

CONTENTS

Mozambican school-
children stand in a
Portuguese colonial
doorway.

3

A Catholic cathedral in Maputo, the capital of Mozambique.

INTRODUCTION

IN 2005 VISITORS TO the British Museum in London stood in awe before an exhibit placed just inside the main entrance. The exhibit was a sculpture of a tree, with small animals and birds busying around it. What made people stare in wonder was that this "Tree of Life" was made entirely of recycled gun parts. The weapons and ammunition clips were the legacy of a brutal civil war that had ravaged Mozambique from 1977 to 1992. A small group of Mozambique artists created the sculpture in 2004 as a statement of their country's determination to build a nation of peace and hope, rising out of the ruins of war.

When Mozambique gained its independence from Portugal in 1975, the future looked promising. It was already a popular destination for tourists drawn to the white-sand beaches and abundant wildlife. But in a matter of months, the country was torn by a vicious civil war. Then, in the midst of rebuilding when peace was established, a flood devastated much of the country, destroying livestock and crops over a wide area.

Today, Mozambique has resumed its reconstruction. Tourists are returning to new, or restored, resorts, cities are bustling, and wildlife is slowly recovering. Two of Mozambique's greatest assets are the determination and hopefulness of its people.

GEOGRAPHY

THE LAND OF MOZAMBIQUE is narrow and elongated, edged by beautiful sand beaches. The white sands, set off by the lush green of palm trees and occasional mangrove swamps, stretch for 1,535 miles (2,470 km) along the southeast coast of Africa.

On a map of the vast continent of Africa, Mozambique looks relatively small and, in fact, 15 other African nations are bigger. But with a land area of 297,846 square miles (771,421 square km), it is three times larger than Great Britain and a little larger than Texas. Much of Mozambique is sparsely populated, and the entire country is far from crowded. Its population of 19,406,703 is about the same as that of New York State, but with only 63 people per square mile, it is no more crowded than the state of Vermont.

Mozambique is bordered on the north by Tanzania and on the northwest by Malawi and Zambia, with Zimbabwe due west. Swaziland and South Africa are located to the south and, on the east, Mozambique faces the Mozambique Channel and the Indian Ocean.

Left: **A white sandy beach, one of many in Mozambique. Mozambique's beaches reflect both the serenity and vitality of the country's coastal areas.**

Opposite: **Lush greenery on the hilly terrain of Mozambique.**

REGIONS

The huge Zambezi River, which flows southeast into the Indian Ocean, forms a decisive dividing line between northern and southern Mozambique. To the south of the river are the lowlands, less than 600 feet (183 m) above sea level. This low-lying plain extends across almost the entire width of the country, except for highlands in the west called the Serra da Gorongosa, which include Mount Binga, the country's highest peak at 7,992 feet (2,436 m).

Villagers walk through a field in rural Maputo.

The southern plain is gently rolling land, interrupted by low hills and by the wide deltas of several rivers. In the extreme south lies Delagoa Bay, the best natural harbor on the entire east coast of Africa. Maputo, the capital of Mozambique, is situated on the bay.

The region north of the Zambezi differs from the south in several ways. Along the coast the sandy stretches are broken up by rocky cliffs and headlands. There are many offshore islands, some of which are coral formations. In addition to the Zambezi, more than 30 rivers flow eastward to the ocean, while the Rovuma River in the far north forms Mozambique's border with Tanzania.

Except for the Serra da Gorongosa, all of Mozambique's higher, more rugged land lies north of the Zambezi. The coastal plain gives way to a higher plateau, and, toward the western borders, the land rises to mountainous terrain, with several peaks above 7,000 feet (2,134 m).

Mozambique is divided into 10 provinces and one capital city (Maputo) with provincial status. Zambezia and Nampula provinces, in the north, have the best farmland and are home to about 40 percent of the people.

By contrast, Maputo and Gaza provinces in the south are thinly populated in the interior.

Although Mozambique is primarily an agricultural nation, with only some 35 percent of the population living in urban areas, there are a number of cities. Only Maputo, formerly known as Lourenço Marques, has a population of 1 million (2 million, including the surrounding area). The other major cities are basically large towns, including Beira, which has a population of 300,000; Nampula, population 250,000; Chimoio, population 177,000; and Quelimane, population 153,000.

The skyline of Maputo, the capital and economic center of Mozambique.

A corn field in Maputo Province, a thinly populated region in Mozambique.

RIVERS AND LAKES

About 50 rivers rise in the mountains west of Mozambique and flow eastward into the Indian Ocean. The Zambezi River, which dominates central Mozambique, is one of the world's largest rivers and the fourth largest in Africa. As it nears the coast, the river becomes as wide as 2 miles (3 km) across.

Both the Ruvuma and Lugenda rivers are important sources of water to the north, providing water for irrigation. South of the Zambezi, the major rivers are the Pungwe, Save (Sabi), Limpopo, and Komati. The Limpopo River is the 10th largest in Africa. Many of Mozambique's older towns were built at the mouths of rivers, as they provided trade routes to the interior. The rivers are useful for canoe travel, but larger modern vessels can only navigate the deeper waters of the Zambezi. Many of the rivers have wide fluctuations in their volume of water between the wet and dry seasons, and the shallow channels often shift course.

Lake Malawi is partly in Malawi and Tanzania, but about one-third of it, or 5,000 square miles (13,000 square km) lie within Mozambique. This dramatically beautiful lake, the third largest in Africa, lies at the southern end of the Rift Valley, the mammoth geological trench that stretches from the Red Sea south through Africa into Mozambique. The lake, formerly known as Lago Niassa, is surrounded by mountains that form the steep slopes of the Rift Valley. The crystal clear waters contain a greater number of indigenous (living naturally in a region) fish species than any other lake in the world. Lake Malawi is also famous for its spectacular sunsets.

Another major lake was formed by the building of the Cabora Bassa Dam. The dam, which was built on the Zambezi River between 1969 and 1974, is the fifth largest in the world, and the lake it created, the Cabora Bassa, covers an area of 1,000 square miles (2,590 square km).

The Limpopo River meanders its way through the south of Mozambique.

THE WONDER OF LAKE MALAWI

The remarkably clear waters of Lake Malawi (*below*) are believed to hold at least 500 species of indigenous fish. That is a greater number of freshwater species than in all of Europe and North America. Some experts believe several hundred more varieties are still to be discovered. A number of species are varieties of cichlids—colorful fish that protect their young by holding them in their mouths until they can take care of themselves.

CLIMATE

Mozambique has a tropical maritime climate, which normally would mean high levels of precipitation. Because of the prevailing winds, however, the moisture generally bypasses Mozambique and rainfall amounts are spotty—high in some areas, very low in others. Maputo, for example, averages only 30 inches (760 mm) of rainfall a year, while the northwest highlands receive as much as 80 inches (2,000 mm) per year. The lack of rainfall sometimes creates severe drought conditions in the south, destroying crops and livestock. Ironically, the overflow of rivers can also lead to flooding, including disastrous floods in early 2000 and early 2001.

In addition to regional variations, rainfall amounts and temperatures fluctuate with the two main seasons: a wet season from November to March, and a longer dry period from April to October. In the southern lowlands January temperatures range from 79°F to 86°F (26°C–30°C), and in the more comfortable dry season, the range is about 20 degrees cooler. The highlands of the north are cooler throughout the year, with January averages of 71°F–77°F (22°C–25°C) and July ranges from 52°F–59°F (11°C–15°C).

Men fishing on a fine day off the coast of Mozambique.

NAMES AND LOCATIONS

Lake Malawi is generally known by that name, and most of its area is within the borders of Malawi. During the colonial period, however, roughly from 1700 to the mid-1900s, it was known as Lake Nyasa and in Malawi it was called Nyasaland. In Mozambique, which was a Portuguese colony, the lake was known as Lago Niassa. These colonial names have remained to this day, so the name of the lake is different from country to country.

VEGETATION

Most of Mozambique's vegetation is savanna (grasslands) and tropical forest. Along the coast, coconut palms are common, with some others, including date palms, also plentiful. Along the well-drained slopes of the hills, there are scattered patches of forest, including stands of ebony and ironwood. Along the upper reaches of the rivers, especially the Zambezi and the Limpopo, the mopani tree, a form of ironwood valued for long-lasting lumber, is common. The most distinct tree of the savanna is the baobab. Stretches of mangrove are found along the coast, while bamboo and spear grass are abundant along the river banks.

An aerial view of the country's arable land and vast countryside.

WILDLIFE

Hunting, poaching, severe drought, and a long civil war have combined to decimate the country's wildlife in some areas, but Mozambique still has a rich and varied fauna. Savanna areas are home to such well-known species as the elephant, rhinoceros, and giraffe, as well as packs of spotted hyena, jackal, and wild dog. Herd animals such as antelope, African buffalo, and zebra are common, as are the predators that stalk them, including cheetahs and lions. Hippopotamuses are common in the lower reaches of the rivers, along with crocodiles. Other abundant species are the warthogs, monkeys, and baboons, plus a variety of snakes, including the cobra, python, puff adder, and viper.

The years of civil war directly affected some areas that were the focus of fighting, including Gorongosa National Park and the land around it.

Elephants are facing a real threat to their existence in Mozambique. Rampant commercial and urban encroachment and relentless poaching and exploitation have dwindled the population of these intelligent animals.

THE BAOBAB TREE

One of the most striking trees in Mozambique is the baobab (*below*). It has a fat, barrel-shaped trunk that can reach 30 feet (9 m) in diameter and short, thin branches, giving rise to the legend that the gods planted it upside down, with its roots thrust in the air.

The baobab has large, gourdlike fruit with a sweet, tasty pulp. People use the strong fiber from the bark to make rope and even cloth, and they sometimes hollow out the trunk for storing water or to use as a temporary shelter. The leaves, when carefully treated, are cooked as vegetables.

MOZAMBIQUE'S MERMAIDS—OR SEA COWS

The dwindling population of the dugong (*below*) has made it one of the most carefully observed creatures of the Bazaruto Archipelago. This large, slow-moving sea mammal is similar to the manatee, a freshwater creature once abundant in the waterways of Florida. Both are related to the elephant.

Like the manatee, the dugong is sometimes called the sea cow because of its slow, grazing movements. Many historians also believe that dugongs (or manatees) are the source of the myth of mermaids.

Several factors contributed to the dangerous decline of dugong populations. Their habitat and feeding ground of sea grass has shrunk, and many are drowned when caught in fishing nets. (They can stay submerged for only about ten minutes.) Also, even though these gentle creatures have a life span of about seventy years, a female gives birth to only one calf at a time and then waits four or five years before having another.

Mozambicans and government officials are determined to protect this endangered species. Aerial surveys are made every year to keep track of habitat and population changes and stiff fines are levied against anyone responsible for the death of a dugong.

A young male cheetah prowls for prey. Poaching is a persistent problem in Mozambique, and It is threatening the rich biodiversity of the country.

The civil war was also destructive because at that time there was no control over poachers. The elephant population, for example, which once numbered more than 54,000, is now only about 15,000.

The country's great numbers of birds were not affected by the civil war, although, as in other countries, human population growth and urbanization are shrinking their habitat. Experts estimate that 850 bird species are either residents or regular migrating visitors to Mozambique, including its offshore islands. About 30 of these species are endemic—they are found only in Mozambique. Many of the birds have colorful names, such as yellow-breasted hylotia, cardinal quela, East African swee, white-tailed blue fly catcher, and Zanzibar red bishop. Bird-watchers have

not fully explored northern Mozambique, so there may be additional varieties that have not been recorded. Of known species in the northeast, large birds include flamingos, cranes, herons, storks, pelicans, and ibis. Deeper inland, quail, guinea fowl, partridge, wild geese, and wild ducks are abundant.

Off the coast of Mozambique, the many islands of the Bazaruto Archipelago feature a wonderful assortment of wildlife. The clear coastal waters are filled with brightly colored fish. Farther out to sea are the migratory routes of humpback whales and bottlenose and humpback dolphins; there are also game fish, such as marlins and sailfish. The islands are also home to 45 species of reptiles and amphibians.

Crocodiles like these are found in islands off the coast of Mozambique.

HISTORY

IN THE YEAR 1498 a Portuguese ship commanded by explorer Vasco da Gama sailed around the Cape of Good Hope, then north to Mozambique Island (off the coast of Nampula). He landed there briefly, claiming it for Portugal. Da Gama then sailed on to India in an historic voyage that opened a trade route between Europe and India, China, and the Spice Islands (modern Indonesia).

At the same time, Christopher Columbus was probing the coasts of the Americas, hoping to find a westward route to those same fabled kingdoms of Asia, with their treasures of silk, ivory, jade, tea, and spices. These great explorations would gradually bring all the world's regions into a global economic network.

Mozambique was soon to play an important part in the emerging international trade. Gold, ivory, and, later, slaves were transported from the interior to the coast, then shipped to distant ports in Europe, Asia, and the Americas. When Vasco da Gama "discovered" Mozambique Island, the region that would become Mozambique already had a long and colorful history.

Opposite: **A monument in Maputo built in commemoration of African and European war veterans who fought during World War I.**

EARLY HISTORY

Many historians and scientists generally agree that the first evidence of human life can be found in the Rift Valley area of Africa. Although there is little fossil evidence in Mozambique, it is safe to say that humans have lived in this region for a million years or more.

Little is known of the early inhabitants—small groups that lived by hunting and gathering food in the wild. By A.D. 100, perhaps earlier, Bantu-speaking groups began moving into the area. The Bantu were sustained by farming and cattle raising. They slowly spread eastward from the highlands, reaching the coast of the Indian Ocean by about A.D. 400.

The Bantu settlements became increasingly complex. Some people became skilled workers and built stone enclosures around their settlements. Several powerful chiefdoms emerged, including the Makua, north of the Zambezi River, and the Karanga in the south.

COASTAL TRADE

Around A.D. 900 Muslim traders began establishing trading posts along the coast of present-day Mozambique. There had long been a prosperous trade along the east coast of Africa, but until A.D. 900 it had not reached so far south. The ancient Egyptians had traded along that northern part of the east coast as early as 2500 B.C. They were later followed by the Phoenicians, Greeks, and Romans. After the fall of the Roman Empire in the fifth century A.D. there was a decline in the coastal trade until Muslims (followers of the religion of Islam) revived it.

The Muslim posts on the coast connected Mozambique to the existing trade routes with the Mediterranean world and also with ports in India and Asia. A town called Sofala, near the mouth of the Buzi River in what is now central Mozambique, became the major trading port. Gold, ivory, iron goods, copper, and cotton were taken from the interior, with the gold from what is now modern-day Zimbabwe (formerly known as Southern Rhodesia) being the most important commodity. Sofala, which no longer exists today, became a prosperous town of about 10,000 people.

Other Muslim commercial settlements also developed north of Sofala. Most of the coastal towns were controlled by Arab sultans, and many of the people had converted to Islam. Caravans carrying cloth, beads, and other goods wound their way up the Zambezi and other rivers into Zimbabwe, returning with gold and other goods to the coast.

A struggle developed for control of this profitable trade. Gradually the cattle-raising Karanga won out in the south while the Makua took control of the north. By about 1100 the trade began to involve slaves from the interior.

THE ARRIVAL OF THE PORTUGUESE

As soon as the king of Portugal learned of the gold trade in Mozambique, he sent expeditions to find out more. By 1502 the Portuguese had made a settlement at Sofala, a gold exporting center, and, in 1507, they occupied Mozambique Island to serve as a way station on trading voyages to India and the Spice Islands. By 1530 they controlled much of the coast, forcing the Muslim traders to relocate.

The Portuguese were eager to reach the source of the gold in Zimbabwe, but they continually encountered stiff resistance from its inhabitants. In 1561 the Shona people killed Gonçalo da Silveira, a Jesuit priest, the head of the first mission in eastern Africa. In response, Portugal sent a large army, which spent the years from 1569 to 1575 trying to conquer the central African gold-mining region. Most of the soldiers died of diseases carried by either mosquitoes or tsetse flies. Of one force of 1,000 men sent out in 1572, for example, only 180 returned.

A statue in Maputo in memory of Portuguese general Mouzinho da Silveira who defeated the Mozambicans in the 19th century.

By the end of the 16th century, consequently, most of Mozambique remained beyond Portuguese control. They occupied the lower Zambezi Valley and established bases at Sena and Tete on the Zambezi River. But the rest of the area remained fragmented.

COLONIAL CLAIM

Until the late 1800s Mozambique was not a Portuguese colony in the usual sense of the word. The Portuguese managed to control a few coastal areas and posts on the Zambezi River, but there never was dominion over a wide area.

Through most of the 17th and 18th centuries Mozambique was a patchwork of small holdings. Some of these holdings were ruled by men who had deserted formal Portuguese settlements. They intermarried with local women, creating a mixed-race group known as *mestiços*. Some *mestiços*, as well as a number of Portuguese settlers, were granted estates by the king of Portugal. These estates, called *prazos*, were given to settlers and wealthy traders and were located mostly in the Zambezi Valley. The rulers of the estates, called *prazeros*, governed with absolute authority, much like the monarchs of feudal kingdoms in Europe during the Middle Ages.

After 1600 Portugal faced sporadic competition from other European countries. In 1607 and 1608 the Dutch made two attempts to take Mozambique Island. Both attacks failed, but they made the Portuguese aware of how insecure and vulnerable their hold on the region was. Consequently they again tried to conquer the interior, and for a time they controlled a large area from the coast inland to the northern part of present-day Zimbabwe. They kept control by granting more *prazos* to

In 1853–64 missionary and explorer David Livingstone explored the Zambezi River and discovered Lake Niassa (now Lake Malawi).

MOZAMBIQUE AND THE SLAVE TRADE

The gold trade declined in the 18th century, but it was replaced by trade with the interior for ivory and for slaves. The slave trade had existed on a small scale even before the arrival of the Europeans. The growth of European-controlled plantations in both the West Indies and East Indies led to a steadily increasing demand for slaves and perpetuated the slave trade, a practice that involved both Africans and Europeans.

Changes in climate affected the slave trade: Mozambique suffered a series of disastrous droughts between about 1790 and the early 1830s; as crops failed and cattle wealth declined, a growing number of people turned to banditry and slave raiding. More and more caravans arrived at the coast with their cargos of chained, frightened villagers from the interior. By 1800 Mozambique was one of the world's major centers of slave trading. Between 1825 and 1830 slaves were shipped from Mozambican ports at the rate of 25,000 per year. While many were sold to plantations in the East Indies, thousands also ended up in Brazil, the West Indies, and the United States.

In 1836, under pressure from Great Britain, the government of Portugal outlawed the slave trade, a move that inadvertently served to drive the cruel activities underground. It is estimated that at least 1 million Africans were shipped from Mozambican ports during the 19th century.

Europeans. (Although modified over time, the *prazo* system of land use continued until the 1930s.) Even though the Portuguese managed to set up armed mining camps, their hold over the interior slowly weakened. In 1693 a chief of the Changamire people led an uprising that forced the Portuguese out of the highlands.

Throughout the 1700s, Portugal struggled to maintain its foothold in Mozambique and to prevent other European powers from moving in. The Portuguese also managed to extend their coastal holdings and, in 1781, permanently occupied Delagoa Bay (at the site of modern Maputo), driving out Dutch and Austrian traders.

MOZAMBIQUE IN THE 19TH CENTURY

The series of droughts that ravaged Mozambique in the late 18th and early 19th centuries provided opportunities for strong African chiefs to gain control over larger areas. The Nguni people became highly militaristic, and three powerful kingdoms emerged: the Zulu, the Swazi, and the Ndandwe. These kingdoms, and other groups in the border region between Mozambique and Zimbabwe, engaged in a series of raids and minor wars through the first half of the 19th century.

THE GAZA EMPIRE

During a prolonged drought in the 1820s, a Nguni chief established a kingdom inland from Sofala. In 1837 he was defeated by another Nguni, named Soshangane, who expanded the kingdom, which became known as the Gaza Empire. At its height in the 1860s, Gaza covered most of southern Mozambique from the Zambezi to the Limpopo rivers. Soshangane also invaded the western highlands north of the Zambezi and established military outposts just outside the modern-day borders of Mozambique, using the posts for raids into the lowlands. After several attempts, Portuguese forces defeated the Nguni, ending the Gaza Empire.

EUROPE'S "SCRAMBLE FOR AFRICA"

In the centuries after the voyages of Christopher Columbus, Vasco da Gama, and other explorers, the countries of Western Europe began building colonial empires in the Americas and Asia. Africa was the last continent to be "carved" into colonies. Throughout the 19th century Europe's great powers took part in a race for colonies that became known as the "Scramble for Africa." Britain led the way and soon controlled a huge swath from Egypt south to the Cape of Good Hope. France, Spain, Germany, Italy, Belgium, and Portugal were all involved in the scramble.

The Portuguese had hoped that they would gain large areas, especially along the coast, on the basis of their many voyages of discovery. But in a series of meetings the European colonial powers used a doctrine called "effective occupation" to grant most large areas to Great Britain. The Berlin Conference in 1884–85 completed the slicing up of the continent, dividing nearly all of it into colonies.

The droughts also destroyed much of the agricultural economy of the Zambezi Valley, driving many *prazeros* to abandon their estates. By the 1850s the region was divided into five large feudal estates ruled primarily by *mestiço* families. Like the feuding kingdoms of the highlands, the valley families bickered and fought with each other and with the Portuguese colonial government.

Throughout much of the century Portugal also struggled to prevent Mozambique from falling into British hands. In the early 1800s the British took control of Cape Colony and then tried to seize the southern portion of Delagoa Bay. Portugal objected and so did the Boer Republic (now the Republic of South Africa). In 1875 France served as arbitrator in the dispute and gave the entire bay to Portuguese Mozambique. After a few more years of arguing, Britain and Portugal signed a treaty in May 1891, giving Mozambique its modern geopolitical shape, although the British gained large areas of the highlands, which are now part of Zimbabwe.

Another 19th-century development was Portugal's invitation to European companies to start plantations to cultivate sugar cane and cotton, and grow sunflower seeds (for oil). These concessions stimulated the Mozambican economy, providing money for improvements in vital infrastructure such as roads and ports. The growing number of European companies also helped to counter British influence in the area.

The former headquarters of Portugal's secret police during the years of Portuguese colonial rule in Mozambique.

THE COLONIAL PERIOD, 1895–1975

Beginning in 1895 with the conquest of the Gaza Empire, Portugal exercised increasing control over Mozambique. Large areas of the country, however, were administered by two large private corporations: the Mozambique Company and the Niassa Company. The companies often forced indigenous workers to labor under brutal conditions, and more than 10,000 were sent each year to work in the gold mines of South Africa.

During the early years of the 20th century, Portugal made sporadic attempts to create unified control over the colony. The city of Lourenço Marques (modern Maputo) was established as the capital of Mozambique, replacing Mozambique Island. And in 1917 an uprising by the Makonde people in Zambezia Province was crushed after bitter fighting. This marked the end of ethnic resistance to Portuguese rule.

Private companies continued to dominate Mozambique until 1926, when a revolution in Portugal led to the rise of a fascist dictator, António de Oliveira Salazar. Salazar ruled Portugal with an iron fist as prime minister from 1932 to 1968. He brought company rule to an end and established direct and centralized control over all of Mozambique.

Salazar established a "planned economy," in which Portugal would be the source of manufactured goods and Portugal's colonies would produce food and raw materials. Company powers were eliminated, and the system of *prazos* was ended. Forced labor was replaced by forced agricultural systems, in which farmers were told precisely what crops to grow. This led to a tremendous increase in the production of rice and cotton between 1930 and 1950.

Portugal remained neutral during World War II (1939–45) and enjoyed considerable prosperity through the export of food and raw materials. After the war Salazar softened his fascist policies. Some industries were developed, and Mozambique's beaches and wildlife began to draw tourists, especially from South Africa.

The increase in Mozambique's exports did not produce a significant change in the standard of living of the people, however. In the planned economy, little attention was paid to crops needed for subsistence and the practice of shipping workers to the South African mines continued. Salazar also encouraged white settlers to move into southern Mozambique, and, partly as a result, the number of white settlers increased to roughly 200,000.

THE MOVEMENT FOR INDEPENDENCE

In the years following World War II, Europe's colonies in Africa were rocked with demands for independence. Many of the movements were started by veterans who had served in the Allied military forces during World War II, when they fought to free people from the tyranny and atrocities of Nazi Germany. Throughout the 1960s and 1970s country after country won its independence.

The movement for independence began late in Mozambique, probably because Portugal had remained neutral in the war, so there were no veterans of the Portuguese military returning to Mozambique. In 1962 a group of exiled Mozambicans met in Tanzania, where they formed an organization called the Front for the Liberation of Mozambique (Frelimo). Its leader was Eduardo C. Mondlane, a Mozambican scholar who had been living in the United States.

Once Portugal refused to negotiate independence, Frelimo decided on guerrilla warfare. By late 1965 Frelimo troops had gained control of large areas in the north. The Portuguese government retaliated, arresting 1,500 Frelimo agents and driving the movement out of the south. At the same time, the government launched a major development program. Jobs were created by the start of the construction on the mammoth Cabora Bassa Dam. The building of roads, schools, and hospitals also stimulated economic growth and, it was hoped, increased loyalty to Portugal.

In spite of Portugal's efforts, Frelimo continued its activities, at least in the north. In 1969 a letter bomb killed Mondlane, and the movement's military commander, Samora Machel, took over as party president in May 1970.

Machel continued the war for liberation. When Portugal sent an additional 35,000 troops, Frelimo returned to guerrilla warfare, including the disruption of work on the Cabora Bassa Dam. How much these activities contributed to Mozambique's eventual independence is uncertain, because the matter was finally decided by events in Portugal. Salazar's health failed in 1968, and a struggle for control followed into the early 1970s. A left-wing military revolution in 1974 produced a new Portuguese government that had no interest in maintaining colonies. Frelimo, headed by Machel, became increasingly influential in Mozambique. In September 1974 Mozambique was granted its independence. A transitional government, with Machel as president, was installed and Mozambique became officially independent on June 25, 1975.

CIVIL WAR, 1977–92

Frelimo assumed power in a one-party government that had no experience in self-government. Samora Machel was president from 1975 until his death in a plane crash in 1986. He had tried to establish a Marxist government with dictatorial powers similar to the governments of the former Soviet Union and other Communist states.

Machel and Frelimo had little chance for success for several reasons. Many educated people and skilled workers had left the country rather than stay in a Marxist society. In addition the world economy was in chaos following the oil crisis of 1973. Perhaps the most serious obstacle to success was Frelimo's support of liberation movements by blacks in Southern Rhodesia (now Zimbabwe) and South Africa. In retaliation the white governments of Rhodesia and South Africa, along with anti-Communist groups in the United States and Europe, tried to undermine Frelimo's control. They formed a militant force of their own called the Mozambican National Resistance, or Renamo. In 1977 Renamo launched a bloody civil war that devastated Mozambique for the next sixteen years.

A landmine, left over from Mozambique's civil war, is detonated near Beline in the south of the country. There is an ongoing effort to destroy or defuse the thousands of unexploded mines speckled through-out Mozambique.

The name Renamo *came from the Portuguese* Resistencia Nacional Moçambicana.

In spite of increasing opposition and violence, the Frelimo government had some success, particularly in social matters. A major education program was started to overcome the country's literacy rate of less than 5 percent. Attendance in primary schools doubled and increased sevenfold in secondary schools. Although there were only 100 trained doctors in the entire country, a massive immunization program reached 90 percent of the population within five years. Another significant change was in promoting the rights of women. In the 1977 elections for popular assemblies, 28 percent of the seats were won by women, one of the highest rates in the world.

The Frelimo government could not overcome the powerful Renamo force, however. In 1980 Renamo began destroying schools, factories, railroads, and government installations. Within a few years the government had undisputed control only over a few cities and travel became increasingly dangerous. Bands of guerrillas roamed the countryside, raiding villages to meet their daily needs.

With tens of thousands of his country's citizens killed and the economy in ruins, President Machel met with the presidents of Zimbabwe and Zambia in 1986, hoping to end some of the outside support for Renamo. On the return flight to Maputo, it was reported that Machel's plane was diverted by a South African radio signal and crashed in South African territory under very suspicious circumstances, killing the president. He was succeeded by Joaquim Chissano, who was elected by Frelimo as Mozambique's new president.

In 1990 Frelimo adopted a new constitution, ending the party's Marxist policies and allowing multiparty elections. The civil war dragged on until 1992, however, until a meeting known as the Rome Conference led to a cease-fire and a peace agreement being signed between President Chissano and the Renamo leader, Alfonso Dhlakama. The killing and destruction had finally ended, but Mozambique lay in ruins and the future did not look very bright.

MODERN MOZAMBIQUE

Mozambique's first democratic elections were held in October 1994. President Chissano won 53 percent of the vote and Dhlakama 34 percent, with the two parties dividing the seats in the parliament, called the Assembly of the Republic, or National Assembly. A United Nations (UN) force, ONUMOZ, entered the country to ensure the peace and to oversee the elections. ONUMOZ completed its work and left the country in early 1995.

Chissano's government faced the Herculean task of rebuilding the economy while reintegrating 1.7 million refugees into the country along

DAVID LIVINGSTONE

A Scottish missionary and explorer, David Livingstone (1813–73) made three extraordinary journeys to the interior of Africa, launching his daring ventures from the mouth of the Zambezi River in Mozambique. In the mid-1850s he made his way up the Zambezi and crossed the continent to Luanda (in present-day Angola) on the Atlantic Coast. To get his party of Mozambicans back to their homes, he retraced his route across Africa. His last expedition included a search for the source of the Nile River. He was found, sick and starving, by American journalist Henry M. Stanley (1841–1904), who was sent by his newspaper to explore rumors that Livingstone was dead. Stanley is said to have uttered the famous line, "Dr. Livingstone, I presume." After exploring together for a while, Stanley returned to Western society. Livingstone continued his work for another year and died at his camp, still exploring and writing.

Livingstone's 30 years of exploration and missionary work had a powerful affect on the West's knowledge of Africa and attitudes toward its people. He also campaigned vigorously for an end to the slave trade. He also helped the West see the potential of people's abilities to form and manage their own nations. In this way he introduced the idea of African nationalism.

Dr. Livingstone's writings about his discoveries in geography, technology, medicine, and social organization provided a storehouse of information that is still being used by modern researchers. Probably no other individual has had so great an influence on Western attitudes toward Mozambique and the rest of Africa.

with thousands of former soldiers from both sides in the long civil war. With considerable foreign aid, the government made slow but steady progress in national reconstruction.

Economic reconstruction received another severe blow in February 2000 when Mozambique experienced one of the worst floods in its modern history. After a month of heavy rain and a cyclone, the rivers in southern and central regions overflowed their banks. Seven hundred people died in the floods and roughly half a million were left homeless. The partially restored roads, bridges, and railway lines were again destroyed, and about 80 percent of the livestock died. The flood also dislodged hundreds of land mines laid during the war and randomly deposited them elsewhere.

Since 2000 Mozambique has again been rebuilding itself. Chissano, who was reelected in 1999, stepped down as president in 2004, and Armando Guebuza was elected to succeed him. The people and the Guebuza government continue their heroic struggle for a decent standard of living, although in 2005 Mozambique was still listed as one of the world's poorest countries.

GOVERNMENT

DURING ITS FIRST 30 YEARS of independence, Mozambique faced extraordinary obstacles. The leaders of the Frelimo independence movement who formed the first government in 1975 had no previous experience in political matters. When the Portuguese granted Mozambique independence, they had allowed for only a nine-month transition period to self-rule—hardly enough time to prepare to run a country.

Frelimo formed a one-party state committed to building a Marxist, or Communist, society similar to the former Soviet Union. This determination led many business owners and others to leave the country rather than live in a Communist society.

The most serious obstacle to the establishment of a stable and successful government in Mozambique was the opposition of anti-Communist groups based outside Mozambique. These resistance groups formed the National Resistance Movement, or Renamo. They received funds and military training from the white-controlled governments of Rhodesia (Zimbabwe) and South Africa. In 1977 Renamo's guerrilla tactics plunged the country into the disastrous civil war that plagued Mozambique until 1992.

THE SEARCH FOR STABILITY

The first important steps to a more democratic government were taken in 1990 when Frelimo unveiled a new constitution that abandoned the party's experiment in communism and provided for multiparty elections. In the elections of 1994 and 1999 President Joaquim Chissano defeated the Renamo leader Alfonso Dhlakama in a close vote, winning with only a

Above: **For the last time as president of Mozambique, Joachim Chissano casts his vote in the 2004 general and presidential elections. Chissano stepped down from the presidency after 18 years in office.**

Opposite: **A statue of Mozambique's revolutionary leader Samora Machel in Maputo's Tunduru Botanical Gardens.**

4 percent margin in 1999. Frelimo also kept its majority in parliament, the 250-member National Assembly, with 133 of the seats in 1998. Renamo claimed that the counting of the votes had been fraudulent. Foreign observers and the Mozambique Supreme Court, however, declared that the elections had been legitimate.

The Chissano government continued to face great difficulties. The enormous damage from the civil war would require years to repair. Moreover, Mozambique faced one of the largest repatriations in African history as 1.7 million refugees returned from having sought asylum in the neighboring countries of Malawi, Zimbabwe, Swaziland, Zambia, Tanzania, and South Africa. Another 4 million Mozambicans who had been internally displaced by warfare or drought returned to their homes in the late 1990s, further swelling the impoverished population. The disastrous flooding in 2000 and 2001 compounded all the existing problems.

The year 2004 was important for Mozambique. In the December elections, President Chissano decided to step down, and his party's handpicked successor, Armando Guebuza, was elected president. Frelimo also won easily in the parliamentary elections, gaining nearly two-thirds of the seats in the National Assembly. Luisa Diogo was appointed prime minister, the first Mozambican woman to attain such a high office.

The Guebuza-Diogo government took office early in 2005, facing the monumental task and gargantuan challenge of rebuilding the still-shattered economy. Economic problems in Zimbabwe and South Africa have added yet another dimension to Mozambique's difficulties. Nevertheless, observers at the polling sites in December 2004 reported an almost-universal upbeat mood. As one United Nations official commented, "The Mozambicans are remarkable. They refuse to give up and they are confident they can build a better future."

THE BRANCHES OF GOVERNMENT

The executive branch of the government is headed by the president, who is both the head of state and the commander in chief. The president is responsible for seeing that legislation is enforced, and he has the power to dissolve the legislature, call for new elections, declare war, and oversee the military. The president is directly elected for a term of five years. Every citizen 18 years or older is eligible to vote.

The prime minister is appointed by the president and is officially the head of government. Prime Minister Luisa Diogo presides over the Council of Ministers—the executive cabinet—in which each minister is in charge of specific governmental departments, such as Finance, Transportation, and Education. The prime minister also submits government programs, such as the annual budget, to the assembly.

UTURO • YO SOY ...UTURO • I AM YOUR FUTURE • JE SUIS VOTRE AVENIR • ستقبلكم

A Mozambican security officer patrols a street in Maputo during the second African Union summit on July 11, 2003. The summit provided a platform for African leaders to examine and resolve the continent's conflicts.

The legislative branch consists of a one-house (unicameral) parliament, officially called the Assembly of the Republic, or National Assembly. The 250 members are elected by popular vote for terms of five years. These members represent Mozambique's 10 provinces plus Maputo, the capital, through a system of proportional representation, in which voters cast their votes for a list of candidates representing political parties or coalitions of parties. The assembly has the authority to veto, or block, some of the president's actions, a power that is balanced by the president's authority to dissolve the assembly before the end of its term.

The judicial branch is headed by the Supreme Court, which is composed of seven justices appointed by the president and 17 elected by the assembly. The Supreme Court oversees the work of the lower courts.

Local government is in the hands of provincial assemblies in each of Mozambique's 10 provinces and in Maputo, the capital. The executive function is carried out by a governor in each province. Governors are appointed by the ruling national party.

POLITICAL PARTIES

For the first 17 years of Mozambique's independence, the only legal party was the ruling Frelimo. After the 1990 constitution provided for a multiparty system, 14 political parties took part in the legislative elections. Nonetheless, Frelimo and Renamo have remained the two dominant parties. Several small parties joined Renamo, with the revised name Renamo-UE (Electoral Union).

DEFENSE

In 1994 Mozambique disbanded its Frelimo-dominated army as part of the peace process ending the 16-year civil war. A new army was recruited from both Frelimo and Renamo soldiers. As of 2006, the army numbered about 8,200 troops, composed mostly of Frelimo recruits. There is also a small navy for coastal patrol to stop poachers and smugglers.

MOZAMBIQUE AND ITS NEIGHBORS

In the early years of the republic, Mozambique had serious problems with its neighbors, especially South Africa and Rhodesia. The Frelimo government supported black independence movements in both countries. Those white-dominated governments retaliated by providing funding, weapons, and training for the Renamo guerrilla force, which plunged Mozambique into the disastrous civil war that raged from 1977 to 1992.

Once South Africa and Zimbabwe (formerly Southern Rhodesia) established governments with black majorities, Mozambique's relations with both countries improved dramatically. Today Mozambique and South Africa enjoy a close relationship, with strong economic ties. Since the end of Mozambique's civil war, the country's beaches and wildlife areas have drawn an increasing number of South African vacationers.

ECONOMY

MOZAMBIQUE HAS FACED tremendous hardships in its first 30 years as an independent nation. A main cause of economic chaos was the determination of the Frelimo government to create a Marxist society, one in which the state owned businesses and property. These efforts angered the owners of Mozambique's industries, most of whom were Portuguese. They fled the country, leaving Mozambique without the expertise or the capital needed to keep businesses operating. (The number of Portuguese living in Mozambique dropped from an estimated 250,000 in 1975 to about 15,000 in the late 1980s.)

The 15-year civil war, combined with the hostility of neighboring countries, left the nation's economy in ruins. As Renamo bands raided the country from Rhodesia and South Africa, they destroyed dams and bridges, tore up railroad tracks, and burned villages. Recovery efforts were in full swing when the floods in 2000 and 2001 set the country back again.

In dealing with the enormous task of rebuilding, Mozambique has great potential. There is plenty of good agricultural land, for example. In fact, about 88 percent of the arable land remains uncultivated. There are also many stands of valuable hardwoods that could provide income for years if harvested wisely. In addition, Mozambique has plentiful natural resources, modern ports, and rail connections to all parts of south central Africa, while the coast and islands have tremendous potential for tourism.

AGRICULTURE

The nation's economy is based on agriculture, and it is this sector that can best be developed first in order to lift Mozambique out of poverty. Mozambique's farms currently account for about 25 percent of the

Above: **Besides killing and displacing thousands of Mozambicans, the devastating floods and heavy rains in 2000 and 2001 also destroyed many roads and other vital infrastructure in the cities of Mozambique.**

Opposite: **Wharves and commercial buildings in the bustling city of Maputo. In recent years Mozambique's economy has been uplifted by a substantial growth in trade and exports.**

Corn plantations dot the land of Mozambique, where subsistence farming is the mainstay of the economy. Corn, like sugarcane, soy, and cassava, is an important and valuable cash crop in the country.

country's gross domestic product (GDP) and about 80 percent of the population relies on farming and fishing to survive.

The major subsistence crops, the crops people depend on for their daily food, include cassava, corn, and rice, which are grown on the flood plains of the many rivers. The most important exports are shrimp and prawns from the offshore waters. Crops grown for export include cotton, cashew nuts, sugarcane, and copra.

Mozambique is making progress in increasing food production, but it is still struggling to get back to self-sufficiency. The country continues to suffer from the loss of crops and 400,000 head of cattle in the 2000 and 2001 floods.

INDUSTRY

Throughout most of the colonial period, Portugal showed little interest in developing Mozambique's industries out of fear that they would create unfair competition for Portuguese industries at home because of lower labor costs. That changed in 1950, and thousands of Portuguese settlers migrated to Mozambique to take advantage of the emergence of a new business climate. Between 1950 and 1975 industry developed rapidly, focusing mostly on processing sugar, copra, tea, and other agricultural products. One goal of the industrial planners was to provide an array of consumer goods for the growing cities, including beer and soft drinks, radios, and furniture. The only heavy industry was the refining of crude oil.

This industrial base was destroyed in the civil war, and the business owners or managers fled the country. When peace was restored in 1992, the Frelimo leaders wisely abandoned their Marxist plans and began a rapid return of businesses to private owners. Businesses that received foreign aid or investment have recovered quickly since. Most of the new industries deal with food processing or the manufacture of furniture and other goods for domestic use.

TRADE AND FOREIGN INVESTMENT

The future health of Mozambique's economy will depend on how much foreign investment is drawn to the country. In the past foreign investment and revenue inflow were drawn in three areas: the transportation of agricultural products to ports on the Indian Ocean; the sending of more than 100,000 workers each year to work in the South African gold mines; and tourism, mostly from South Africa.

Transportation systems were severely damaged during the civil war, but they are gradually being restored, so the shipping of agricultural products is returning to preindependence levels. The arrangement for sending workers to South Africa and Southern Rhodesia was ended by Mozambique in the early 1980s. From 1928 to 1980 the exporting of workers was very profitable for Mozambique. Sixty percent of each worker's wages

Cassava, a root vegetable also known as manioc, is native to South America. Mozambique grows more of it than any other country in Africa. Copra is the white, meaty part of the coconut. Its main use is to make coconut oil, widely used for baking and cooking. Coconut oil cakes are also used as cattle feed, and dried and shredded coconut meat is used in Europe and North America primarily for baking.

was paid to the government in gold. Mozambique then sold the gold on the world market for a profit. In 1975 alone the government earned $150 million from a labor pool of 103,000 workers.

In spite of the civil war setbacks, Mozambique has the potential to attract large amounts of foreign investment. First, the government has established "industrial free zones" in the major cities. In these areas, some of the taxes are waived as an incentive to foreign business.

Another area for growth is in a number of "transportation corridors" that link the coast to the interior of the continent. These corridors are rail lines that extend from neighboring countries across Mozambique to such seaports as Maputo and Beira.

Foreign companies are awarded licenses to maintain the country's railroads and port facilities. For example, a consortium of American and Portuguese companies operates the Malawi-Nacala Railroad and the port at Nacala.

There is also hope in the huge Cabora Bassa hydroelectric plant on the Zambezi River. Severe damage caused during the civil war was repaired and the plant resumed limited operation in 1997. Combining this with another plant downriver that is nearing completion, the government expects to increase its foreign earnings by selling electricity to neighboring countries. In November 2005 Portugal and Mozambique finally resolved their dispute over the control of proceeds from the operation of the Cabora Bassa dam. It was agreed that Portugal would receive 15 percent and Mozambique 85 percent of the proceeds.

NATURAL RESOURCES

During the colonial period the Portuguese government paid little attention to Mozambique's mineral deposits. In fact, no one knew what enormous resources the colony did have. Mozambique's hidden wealth of natural

A natural gas processing plant in the province of Inhambane in Mozambique.

resources were therefore not fully tapped. Explorations made between 1977 and 1983 were more extensive than all those made during the entire colonial period.

The investigations revealed that Mozambique has rich deposits of coal, iron ore, salt, and phosphate, along with smaller amounts of gold, tantalum, chromium, copper, bauxite, and nickel. Later explorations have also caused much excitement. In 1999 the largest reserve of titanium in the world was discovered in Gaza Province, and natural gas was found in Inhambane Province at the same time.

As with the hopes for industry, the development of any of these resources will require a lot of foreign investment. By early 2005 only coal and salt were being mined, but bauxite and titanium were beginning to be exploited. The Moma titanium project is being operated by a company from Ireland. A very hopeful sign has been the opening of Mozambique

Aluminum (MOZAL), the most ambitious foreign-investment project in Mozambique, which now employs nearly 1,000 people.

FORESTRY AND FISHING

Mozambique continues to have good stands of trees, including potentially valuable hardwoods. In common with other African nations, however, rural people are cutting trees at a rapid rate and burning the wood for fuel, not for timber. Of the 635 million cubic feet (18 million cubic m) of forest cut in 2001, less than 1 million cubic feet (0.028 cubic m) was used for lumber.

Fishing is important for the coastal and island communities, and shellfish are the largest export commodity. In addition, fish form a significant part

CABORA BASSA DAM

Situated on the Zambezi River in the north of Tete Province, Cabora Bassa Dam is the fifth largest in the world and creates one of the 10 largest lakes in Africa. The name Cabora Bassa means "where the work ends"—a phrase in a local dialect that means that canoes could not go any farther up the rapids. Construction on the mammoth concrete wall began in 1969 and was completed in 1974, although Frelimo tried to sabotage the project by initiating a guerilla offensive. The power plant was damaged during the civil war when Renamo destroyed the main power line.

Cabora Bassa, when operating at full capacity, can produce 10 times the amount of electricity needed for Mozambique. That means that a great deal of this valuable product can be sold to the country's power-hungry neighbors. An obstacle was created by a 1970s contract that allows Portugal to own 82 percent of the hydroelectric company, and Portugal has been insisting that most of the power be sold to South Africa. Castigo Langa, Mozambique's Minister of Mineral Resources and Energy, said recently that "it is no longer acceptable that the dam is not being used for the Mozambican people." The stumbling block was that the power company still owes Portugal $2 billion for the construction of the dam. In November 2005 Mozambique reached an agreement with Portugal by which the debt will be paid by giving Portugal 15 percent of the revenues produced by the dam.

Fishing off the coast of Mozambique.

of the diet for Mozambican families throughout the country. Fortunately, Mozambique's lakes and rivers have large fish populations, with tilapia being the most popular catch.

TOURISM

Before independence and the civil war, Mozambique had been a popular destination for tourists. Visitors from South Africa and the landlocked countries enjoyed the beach resorts. Tourism went into a steep decline from 1976 to the mid-1990s. While 292,000 visitors went to Mozambique in 1972, this figure dwindled to about 1,000 each year in the 1980s. By the year 2000, tourism was again the fastest growing sector of the economy.

Early in 2000 the Mozambique government created the Ministry of Tourism, which oversees a program called the National Policy of Tourism,

An antelope splashes across the Futi River off the Maputo Elephant Reserve.

setting priorities for the near future. Top priority was given to restoring and expanding the beach resorts near Maputo and Beira. A major rehabilitation project is also underway at Gorongosa National Park, which had been the most-visited wildlife area.

Mozambique's wildlife could attract tourists to the country's six national parks and five game reserves. The tourism potential differs for each of these wildlife centers and so also do the government's plans.

Niassa National Reserve, on the border with Tanzania, is being promoted as a low-key, off-the-beaten-path destination. Visitors who do not mind roughing it out can still encounter a wide array of mammals and birds. A more ambitious plan calls for restocking the Maputo Special Reserve (formerly the Maputo Elephant Reserve), on the coast south of the capital, and combining safaris with beach vacations on Inhaca Island

and Ponta d'Ouro. In order to improve and expand access to wildlife areas, the government has worked with South Africa to tear down the fence between Banhine National Park and Kruger National Park in South Africa. This has created the jointly managed Transfrontier Wildlife Park, also known as the "Peace Park," which is one of the largest wildlife reserves in the world.

Another reemerging tourist attraction is sport fishing off Benguerra Island. Game fish caught in the Bazaruto Archipelago area includes striped marlins, some weighing up to 800 pounds. Sailfish are caught throughout the year, as are bonito, king and queen mackerel, giant barracuda, and

A tourist shops for some local handmade items at Maputo's Saturday craft market. Handmade ceramic vases, intricate carvings, and paintings with stylized motifs are also exhibited along beachfronts for sale to tourists.

several kinds of kingfish. Experts offer saltwater fishing lessons and demonstrations to tourists, and other specialists give lessons on diving in the waters around the spectacular and unspoiled coral reefs.

HOPES FOR THE FUTURE

Mozambique has experienced steady economic improvement since 1994. There are several indicators of improvement: although inflation was high during the civil war, it has generally been below 10 percent since then; more than 1,200 state-owned businesses, mostly small ones, have been returned to private owners; the economy has been growing at a rate of between 7 and 10 percent each year; the gross domestic product (GDP) per person was about $120 per year in the mid-1980s and has risen to an estimated $1,200 in 2004.

While the signs of progress are encouraging, the country still faces huge problems. The per person GDP of $1,200 continues to place Mozambique among the world's poorest countries. One of the most serious problems is Mozambique's trade imbalance—importing more than it exports. Imports each year were often four times greater than exports, so that by 1999 Mozambique owed a staggering $4.8 billion.

Several measures have helped to reduce Mozambique's debt. Both the International Monetary Fund (IMF) and the World Bank have ruled that, because of its high rate of poverty, it is eligible for "debt forgiveness," allowing the nation to pay far less than it owes. In 2005 Mozambique was listed as one of the few developing countries whose debt would be completely forgiven. New projects like the exporting of electric power and the development of the titanium processing plant will also help. While the trade imbalance persists, it is less now than in the past. In 2001 imports cost the country $1.6 billion, while exports amounted to $703 million.

Mozambique will continue to rely on international aid and foreign investment to develop a truly healthy economy. At least all the economic indicators appear to be headed in the right direction. What is more, the government no longer has to devote so much energy and money to correcting the massive damage created by the civil war and the floods; more attention can now be devoted to diversifying the economy, developing industry, and reducing poverty.

Above: **A bustling street market in Maputo. Mozambique's economy is dependent on exports and tourism.**

Opposite: **Two teenage Mozambican boys sell plastic bags in Maputo.**

ENVIRONMENT

MOZAMBIQUE IS A BEAUTIFUL country of gently rolling hills, dozens of sparkling rivers, seemingly endless miles of white-sand beaches, with brilliantly clear waters in its lakes and around the offshore islands. Wildlife shares the land with hundreds of small villages, where subsistence farming rarely causes serious environmental damage. The country is not experiencing the kinds of environmental problems that plague most nations—problems such as land, air, and water pollution, population pressures, or urban sprawl.

Mozambique does face serious environmental and conservation issues, however. For instance, its once abundant wildlife has been severely reduced, devastated by the 15 years of civil war and rampant poaching that could not be controlled during the fighting. The country's elephant population, for example, has been reduced from more than 55,000 in 1980 to about 15,000 today.

Left: **An oilspill off the coast of Mozambique.**

Opposite: **An aerial view of Mozambique still submerged in flood-waters after relentless rains that led to widespread devastation, and the tragic loss of lives in 2000.**

Above: **Houses, shops, roads, and other vital infrastructure in Xai-Xai Province are ravaged by heavy rains.**

Opposite: **An aerial view of a part of Gorongosa National Park.**

Environmental issues have also contributed to widespread public health problems. Lack of sanitation facilities and poor personal hygiene lead to a variety of communicable diseases, which claim thousands of lives every year.

Mozambique's leaders and many of its people are working hard to address these issues. They know that the country's economic future can be greatly improved if tourists are drawn to its many wildlife areas. And steps are being taken to reduce the environmental causes of illness.

WILDLIFE CONSERVATION

Mozambique's leaders are determined to restore the country's wildlife areas to their pre-civil war abundance, then to protect those areas from poachers and make them attractive to tourists. It is a monumental task, especially in the areas where the destruction was greatest. Here are examples of the progress being made and the difficulties that persist.

The disastrous floods that hit Mozambique at the turn of the century have exacerbated the environmental crisis faced by the local people. Mozambicans have had to grapple with the severe lack of safe drinking water and the appalling sanitary conditions in the country.

GORONGOSA NATIONAL PARK Officially called the Parque Nacional da Gorongosa, this park was once the most popular of Mozambique's wildlife reserves and received more than 12,000 visitors a year. It was considered one of the best in Africa, with far more wildlife than neighboring Kruger National Park in South Africa. But Gorongosa was hard hit by the civil war. The Renamo military set up its headquarters near Mount Gorongosa just outside the park. Fighting in and around the park was almost constant and much of the area was heavily mined.

Large numbers of wild animals were killed during the fighting, but no species was totally destroyed. As soon as the shooting stopped, wildlife

Elephants are killed by poachers for their ivory tusks, which are very valuable. Rhinoceros are poached because rhino horns are highly prized in parts of Asia, where some people believe the horns have magical powers of rejuvenation.

numbers slowly started to climb, and the antipoaching measures seem to be very effective. A growing herd of elephants, currently numbering about 75, roams the park, and sightings of African buffaloes and lions have increased.

Park officials have worked hard to restore the tourist facilities and trails. They hope that wildlife numbers can be brought back without expensive restocking. Gorongosa National Park may again be the country's most popular wildlife area, but it will take many years for its flora and fauna to reach pre-civil war levels.

BANHINE NATIONAL PARK The interior of Gaza Province in southern Mozambique is an arid region, thinly populated, seeming to have very little to offer foreign visitors. But an interesting experiment is underway at Banhine National Park, a small wildlife area that has received few visitors until now. The experiment has involved tearing down the fence that separates Banhine from South Africa's Kruger National Park.

The new park, called the Transfrontier Wildlife Park, is already one of the largest in the world. Also known as the "Peace Park," it will soon be even larger with the inclusion of Gonarezhou National Park in Zimbabwe. For Mozambique, much will depend on the country's ability to attract tourists to its entrance town of Massingir; otherwise tourists will enter through South Africa or Zimbabwe, reducing the income for Mozambique.

MAPUTO SPECIAL RESERVE This small game reserve was hardly known outside Mozambique, although it is only about a two hour's drive from the nation's capital. In the 1990s an American investor had plans to develop safaris there combined with beach vacations on offshore islands, but he ran out of funds. Since then, poaching has caused heavy damage.

Sixty-five white rhinoceroses were introduced into the park from South Africa in the mid-1990s, but all have been killed. The number of elephants has been reduced from about 350 in 1971 to fewer than 180 in 1994.

A Canadian environmentalist named Maurice Strong has now taken over the project, with plans to restock several species. Cheetahs, leopards, and African buffalo appear to be locally extinct, but Strong's group has plans to restock these and others. So far, access to the reserve is limited by the rough terrain, but new roads are being built, along with tourist facilities such as lodges and restaurants.

MARROMEU GAME RESERVE This reserve at the Zambezi Delta has also suffered severe damage, both from the fighting and from poaching. The number of elephants was reduced from 1,500 to fewer than 300 in just two years, 1988 to 1990. The African buffalo population suffered even more,

MOZAMBIQUE'S NATIONAL PARKS AND GAME RESERVES

National Parks
- Gorongosa National Park, north of the Beira Transportation Corridor
- The Quirimba Archipelago, near the border with Tanzania
- Bazaruto Archipelago, off the coast opposite Vilankulo
- Limpopo, on the Limpopo River, near Zimbabwe border

Game Reserves
- Niassa National Reserve, on the border with Tanzania
- Gilé National Reserve, southeast of Nampula
- Marromeu Game Reserve, at the Zambezi Delta
- Pomene Game Reserve, on the coast between Inhambane and Vilankulo
- Maputo Special Reserve, on the coast, south of Maputo

being reduced from more than 55,000 in the early 1970s to about 4,000 twenty years later. Other species, including hippopotamus, sable, black rhinocerous, and leopard, have been reduced by 80 to 90 percent.

Wildlife specialists and economists agree that Marromeu probably cannot be restored without ambitious restocking. To increase the flow of foreign dollars through tourism, Mozambique also has to build facilities near the entrance to the reserve. Both restocking and building lodges require funds that, so far, are not available.

Mozambique's natural reserves will help protect wildlife such as the rhinoceros from eventual extinction.

MOZAMBIQUE'S COAST AND ISLANDS

One of Mozambique's greatest assets is its Indian Ocean coast, including the offshore islands. The islands that make up the Bazaruto Archipelago fit the ideal image of islands outlined with white-sand beaches and palm trees. The five islands, which were designated a National Park in 1971, were untouched by the civil war; in fact, tourists continued to fly directly to the main island, Benguerra, during the fighting.

Like much of the coast and most islands, these areas have no environmental problems. Instead, they represent tremendous potential for future development. Mozambique's leaders are determined to control growth and tourism and to avoid the environmental nightmare that other countries have experienced.

In spite of its problems with wildlife depletion, Mozambique has the opportunity to develop an economy that lifts all its people above the poverty level. Many men and women in the country's government are convinced that this can be achieved even in a largely agricultural society and without the usual pollution problems faced by emerging nations.

A sea plane on the coast of Mozambique's Bazaruto Archipelago. The country's rich and fascinating marine life is in danger of extinction if pollution in the water off Mozambique is not curbed and environmental regulations are not effectively enforced.

A Mozambican man stands outside his wrecked hut, one of many that were ravaged by heavy rains.

ENVIRONMENT AND HEALTH

One reason that life expectancy is less than forty years in Mozambique is that so many die from diseases that can be controlled or eradicated. In common with other African nations, a tragically large percentage of the population suffers from either malaria or AIDS, sometimes both.

Contaminated food and water, as well as poor personal hygiene, contribute to several serious illnesses, such as hepatitis A, typhoid, cholera, and bilharzia (also called schistosomiasis, or snail fever). Through the expansion of local clinics and aid from a variety of international agencies such as the World Health Organization (WHO) and the Bill and Melinda Gates Foundation, rural Mozambicans are beginning to learn about avoiding contaminated food or water. One of the most serious challenges is getting protection against infectious diseases. According to the United

LAND MINES: A SPECIAL ENVIRONMENTAL PROBLEM

Millions of land mines were laid during the civil war and, according to some estimates, 3 million remained as late as 1999. The tremendous floods in 2000 and 2001 lifted thousands of mines and redistributed them. As late as 2005, visitors were warned not to drive or hike away from standard pathways. United Nations's personnel continue to provide training to local clinics on how to care for land mine injuries.

Nations Development Program, more than 15 percent of Mozambique's adults are HIV positive.

Efforts are also being made to control the mosquito strains that cause diseases like malaria. While there is no cure for malaria, steps are being taken to drain mosquito-breeding swamps and to make the environment safer. Scientists have found, for example, that sleeping under nets sprayed with a long-lasting insecticide can reduce the cases of severe malaria by 70 percent. The nets cost only a few dollars, but buying and distributing them is not easy in a poor country.

A child plays in a pool of stagnant water in the town of Machanga in south Beira.

MOZAMBICANS

THE BITTER CIVIL WAR that devastated Mozambique from 1977 to 1992 had a long-lasting effect on the country's population. In addition to the numbers killed or seriously wounded, nearly 2 million fled to other countries. Entire villages were destroyed, and many skilled workers were murdered. Crops were burned and livestock destroyed, along with roads, bridges, and railroads. A generation of young people grew up without schools or clinics and often without families or homes.

In spite of that long nightmare, the people seem remarkably upbeat and optimistic about the future. Foreign observers all agree that the country has made extraordinary progress over the past 10 years and Mozambique now has one of the fastest growing economies in all of Africa. Another hopeful sign is that the war did not leave a legacy of ethnic bitterness or rivalries that could erupt in renewed violence. Instead, people in every ethnic group seem committed to resolving conflicts peacefully. One of the artists involved in creating sculptures from decommissioned weapons said that villagers everywhere were eager to turn in their weapons in advocation of peace. "People in one village used the money they made to buy an old tractor," he said. "Now they're growing a new cash crop instead of buying more guns and ammunition."

Above: **Three Mozambican teenage friends enjoy a time of leisure and fun with one another.**

Opposite: **A Mozambican girl smiles for the camera.**

AN ETHNIC PATCHWORK

About 99 percent of Mozambique's people are African. The remaining 1 percent is made up of Europeans (mostly Portuguese), with small numbers of Indians, East Asians, and *mestiços* (people of mixed European

Mozambican children excited at the sight of aid workers who arrived to provide food and other essentials to relieve the tragic plight of victims of the flood of 2000.

and African descent). The African population is divided into more than 200 ethnic groups, with diverse languages, culture traits, and histories.

The basic makeup of the population was established by three historical movements of people. First, in A.D. 1000, dozens of Bantu people moved into Mozambique from the north and west. The second migration took place in the early 19th century when thousands fled north from present-day South Africa to escape the violent expansion of the Zulu kingdom. The third, more haphazard movement involved Persians, Arab Muslims, Portuguese, and other non-Africans who settled along the east coast over the past 500 years.

As each new group settled in Mozambique, a basic pattern emerged. The country became divided into two, with the peoples who settled in the north having ways of living quite different from those of the south. The mighty Zambezi River formed the dividing line.

NORTHERN MOZAMBIQUE

Nearly all the ethnic groups in the north live by subsistence farming, although a few also grow some cash crops, while others rely on coastal fishing. Another distinguishing feature of the north is that most societies are matrilineal—that is, they trace descent through the woman's family line.

The two largest northern ethnic groups are the Makua and the Lomwe. Together they make up roughly one-third of Mozambique's population. Both groups migrated from the upper reaches of the Zambezi and settled between Malawi and the coast along the Indian Ocean.

North of the Makua and the Lomwe are two other large ethnic clusters: the Yao and the Makonde. Both groups straddle the Rovuma River, so they have settlements in Tanzania as well as Mozambique. The Makonde, known for their outstanding wood carvings and masks, have traditionally been one of the most conservative societies—that is, resistant to change. While Muslims managed to convert other ethnic groups to Islam, the Makonde kept their traditional beliefs. The Yao, who did convert to Islam, now live in the northwest corner of the country. In the 18th and 19th centuries they were major middlemen in the trade for slaves and ivory.

Two Mozambican women piggy-back their children as they work in the fields.

SOUTH OF THE ZAMBEZI RIVER

The Zambezi Valley was settled by a variety of small ethnic groups and also by Portuguese and other non-Africans. Portuguese landowners operated large estates with African workers who were not much more than slaves.

South of the Zambezi, a number of clans or ethnic groups carved out territory for themselves. These included the Tsonga, Karanga, Shona, Chopi, and Nguni. All were part of eastern Africa's cattle-raising culture. The people lived by farming, but their cattle were the measure of wealth and prestige. The southern societies also differed from the north in being patrilineal—tracing descent through the male line.

The Tsonga, living between the Save River and Delagoa Bay, is the second largest ethnic group in Mozambique, making up about 23 percent of the population. During the years that migrant workers were sent to the gold and diamond mines of South Africa, most were Tsonga.

THE MAKONDE: PROFILE OF AN ETHNIC GROUP

The Makonde are one of the best-known ethnic groups in Mozambique. They are famous throughout Africa for their wood carvings and also for a masked dance known as *mapiko*.

Although many of the Makonde have moved across the border into Tanzania, about 200,000 still live in Mozambique. Like many northern societies, they are matrilineal. Children belong to their mother and so does any inherited property or wealth. It is not unusual for a husband to move to his wife's village.

The Makonde's small settlements are widely scattered, a tradition that began in the 1700s when families often had to flee to avoid slave raids. Even today, each small village remains isolated and independent, ruled by its own chief and council of elders. This isolation also kept them independent of outside influences. Most have clung to their traditional African religion, for example, rather than adopting either Islam or Christianity.

They also form the largest ethnic group in Maputo, the capital. Because so many have worked outside the country and have been exposed to other cultures, they have been more willing than other societies to accept new ideas and change.

Another large group of people, the Shona, forms a majority in Sofala and Manica provinces. The Shona population has been growing because of migrations from South Africa and Zimbabwe.

The many ethnic groups exhibit a spirit of unity in their common desire to build a better Mozambique. And there are similarities in culture, dress, and ways of living. But each society also retains elements of a separate history and culture. Portuguese colonial leaders discovered how strong those traditions can be when they tried to change traditional agricultural systems in the 1930s. Each group found its own way to resist new systems and the Portuguese finally gave up.

NON-AFRICAN PEOPLES

The non-African peoples, consisting of Portuguese and other Europeans, Asians, and *mestiços*, have been few in number, but they have had a powerful influence, especially on the economy.

In 1930 there were only 17,000 whites in Mozambique; nearly all Portuguese. By 1950 the number had grown to about 48,000; this then doubled during the 1950s and reached 250,000 by the time of independence in 1975. The growth of industry and international trade provided incentives for Europeans to come. Many worked in Maputo or Beira, and a small but growing number began building lodges at game reserves and at resorts in the beach areas. The Portuguese tried elaborate settlement schemes in the Zambezi Valley, offering Europeans land and agricultural workers. But only a handful accepted the offer.

Clean drinking water is scarce in many remote areas in Mozambique. Here, villagers in Chokwe draw clean water from a pump donated by Norway.

When Mozambique became independent, and the Communist-leaning Frelimo came into power, the bubble burst. The Portuguese fled almost overnight and, within two years, only 15,000 remained. The flight of the Europeans was devastating to the economy. They had held nearly all the professional and skilled jobs, and many destroyed the facilities they had built rather than see them help a Communist society.

Mozambique is still trying to recover from the chaos created by the departure of the Portuguese and other Europeans. Since 2000 the country's stability and the incentives offered by the government have led to a steady increase in the number of non-Africans. As was the case before independence, most live in Maputo, with lesser numbers in the other cities. British, Germans, white South Africans, and Zimbabweans, and even a few Americans have joined the Portuguese in establishing businesses and professional offices. Small numbers of Chinese, Pakistanis, and Indians have commercial establishments, especially along the coast.

SOCIAL STRATIFICATION

In 1927 the Portuguese colonial government established a rigid system of social stratification that continues to influence Mozambican society today. The system divided the entire population into two categories, or classes: the *indígenas* were the indigenous Africans (sometimes called unassimilated Africans); and the *não indígenas*, consisting of Europeans, Asians, *mestiços*, and assimilated Africans, also called *assimilados*.

The *indígenas*, who made up the majority of the population, had few rights. They had to carry identity passes, obey curfews, and pay taxes. They could also be ordered to serve in labor gangs for private business as well as for public works projects.

A group of nursery school children on a field trip in the capital of Maputo.

The *não indígenas* formed the privileged upper class. They enjoyed full rights of citizenship, and they controlled the economy. Africans could become *assimilados* by meeting several strict requirements. They had to know the Portuguese language and abandon traditional dress and ways of living. They also had to be employed in industry or trade and provide testimonials of their good character.

Many Africans hated this system that made them second-class citizens. Dislike of the system helped to shape Frelimo, establishing the goal of creating a society without social classes.

Right: **A group of young rural Mozambican boys enjoy a good splash in the cool waters off the coast of Mozambique.**

Opposite: **Two young Mozambican siblings pounding wheat in their village compound.**

TOWARD SOCIAL EQUALITY

When Frelimo came to power in 1975, the movement's leaders were determined to create a classless society, based on the Marxist ideal. Mozambique, they declared, would be classless, nonracist, and not ethnically based or segregated by virtue of race. They also wanted it to be an atheistic society.

The Frelimo idealistic program encountered huge obstacles. The leaders did not take into account the diversity of the people or the strength of their traditions. People in many ethnic groups resisted the attempt to create large state-managed farms. Another program, the setting up of farm collectives in consultation with farm workers, was also difficult because, in most societies, the people were accustomed to having the chief make the decisions on behalf of the community. Many people also disliked the effort to close churches and mosques and to reduce the influence of traditional African religions.

In 1990 Frelimo leaders agreed to end their experiment with Communism. This move restored traditional chiefs to the position as the managers and decision makers of their communities. Spiritual leaders also resumed their customary roles and authority.

LIFESTYLE

MORE THAN 80 PERCENT of Mozambique's people depend on subsistence farming, very much as their ancestors had been for centuries. The typical farm village consists of several houses clustered around a cattle *kraal* or a meeting place, such as a school. Fields of crops are scattered outside the village. In some societies each family tends its own plots of farmland; in others all the families work together and share the harvest.

Small cities, most of which began as trading centers, have grown slowly. Maputo, by far the largest city, has been the country's capital only since the late 19th century. City growth was hampered by Portugal's lack of interest in industry until the 1950s and 1960s. When the Europeans fled after independence, Maputo and other cities became hollow shells, and some suffered heavy war damage. Since the fighting ended in 1992, cities have become exciting, growing centers of business and entertainment.

Above: **A doorman of a hotel in Maputo sports pins acquired from tourists from all over the world.**

Opposite: **Mozambican men playing volleyball on the beach of bustling Maputo.**

LIFE IN MAPUTO

Maputo, the bustling, fast-growing capital of Mozambique, is situated on a low bluff overlooking Maputo Bay. With a population of more than 1 million people, it is also the capital of one of the smallest but most densely populated provinces in the country.

This is a busy and attractive port city located where three rivers flow into the Indian Ocean. The growing economy provides an upscale lifestyle for middle-class office workers and store managers. Many city people live in apartment buildings on broad avenues lined with jacarandas, flame trees, and several kinds of palm trees.

The city began as a fishing village some 500 years ago. In the 18th and 19th centuries the city was named Lourenço Marques, and it was known as the "playground of the rich." With the landlocked gold and diamond regions of South Africa and Southern Rhodesia only 70 or 80 miles away, "LM," as it was called, was a natural destination for good food and lively entertainment. Today it is a thriving business center and still an important port, capable of handling 20 oceangoing ships at the same time. And, unlike the apartheid-like restrictions of the past, everyone can now enjoy the city.

Freshly painted office buildings, apartments, restaurants, and stores can be found in most parts of Maputo. In the main business district, called the *baixa*, businesspeople in Western-style clothing talk over lunch or drinks at tree-shaded outdoor cafés. Well-to-do shoppers, many driving Mercedes

The skyline of the port of Maputo.

A Mozambican waiter in Maputo's Polana Hotel.

or BMWs, visit designer shops or the Mercado Central (Central Market), a noisy, lively hodgepodge of stalls selling fruits and vegetables, housewares, and local crafts. The pace is easygoing and relaxed, except at night when pubs, bars, clubs, and discos rock with all kinds of music—Western, Asian, and African—until close to dawn. Attractive residential avenues, lined with houses and apartment buildings, overlook the harbor and bay.

The "old town," closest to the harbor, seems even quieter and more laid back than the business district, and includes many historic buildings. The huge 1910 railroad station attracts many foreign visitors, drawn to the dome designed by Gustave Eiffel, famed for his Eiffel Tower in Paris. Nearby are located the city's oldest mosque and a modern Roman Catholic cathedral. Another Eiffel-designed structure is known as the Iron House. It was intended as a residence for the colonial governor, but the metal walls held in too much of the tropical heat, so the building has been used primarily as a tourist attraction.

There is a good deal of poverty in the capital, but it is generally spread out. Some of the poor live in high-rise buildings left over from the Frelimo era, when the government built monolithic buildings like those in the former Soviet Union. Since few people chose to live in those structures, they became tenements for the poor. Other poor families have built shantytowns on the outskirts of the city.

OTHER CITIES

During the colonial period Portugal invested heavily in roads and railroads to connect coastal ports with the interior and with the prosperous mines and towns of South Africa and Southern Rhodesia (Zimbabwe). As a result, most of Mozambique's cities have developed in the south. Transportation connections to the north are, on the other hand, primitive and slow.

A health worker vaccinates a Mozambican child against measles at a hospital in the town of Xai-Xai in Mozambique.

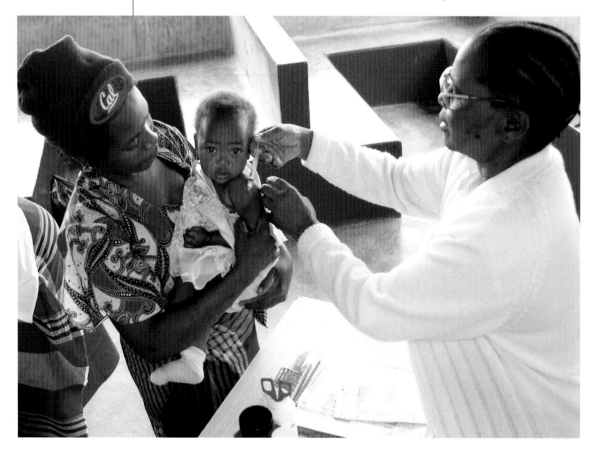

Beira, Mozambique's second largest city, had the reputation of being a tough seaport town. It had begun as a fishing village in the ninth century, and the modern city was not built until after 1880, upon the completion of the transportation corridor. By 1900 it was a rough-and-tumble port with 4,000 people and 80 bars. It was a major port in the gold trade.

Today Beira appears rather tired and rundown, but this city of 300,000 has improved considerably over the past decade. The center of the city is being restored, and people can once again meet at attractive outdoor cafés. In the business district street vendors offer snacks, craft items, and gifts. Beira still has a long way to go to restore the charm of its past. Much poverty remains, and poor people have built shantytowns in the outskirts. Public health, sanitation, and other city services are still in disrepair, but there is hope that foreign investment can speed up the reconstruction.

Public gardens give the city a pleasant, parklike appearance. This is most welcome when the winds off the Indian Ocean turn hot and sticky. A few miles away is the site of the ancient gold-trading town of Sofala. It was once a thriving middle point in the coastal trade, with links to the Persian Gulf kingdoms as well as to India and Indonesia. Sofala has since disappeared, although stones from its fort were used to build the Roman Catholic cathedral in Beira.

Other cities in Mozambique are really large towns. These include Xai-Xai (pronounced Shy-Shy), Inhambane, Quelimane, Angoche, Namaacha, and Nampula. Nampula is the country's third largest city and the commercial center of the north. It is a pleasant, bustling city, with a temperate climate and the long, broad avenues that seem to characterize all of Mozambique's cities. Although the town draws few foreign visitors, it does serve as a transportation crossroads for the whole of north Mozambique and for travel between the coast and Malawi.

As in many large towns, the people in Nampula flock to a lively craft market held every Sunday.

A craft market in Maputo. Vendors display their handmade crafts for sale along the street.

RURAL LIFE

Rural families work hard to scrape together a decent living. Much of the hard work falls on the women, including many thousands who were widowed by the civil war. In addition to raising children, the women are the ones responsible for planting the crops, tending them, and gathering the harvest. They also prepare food for storage or for meals. Even the staple foods require hard work. A basic cornmeal mush, called "porridge," for example, takes a long time to prepare as the corn (maize) needs to be pounded for several hours before it becomes cornmeal. The porridge is then cooked over an open fire.

In spite of the seemingly endless struggle, there is both variety and hope in Mozambique's rural lifestyles. Over the past century there have been several efforts to change rural life, but African traditions have proved stronger than plans created by government authorities. In the 1930s the

Portuguese introduced a system called *shibalo* (from a Swahili word *shiba*, meaning "serf"). Rural people were forced to work on large estates, called *colonatos*, growing cash crops such as cotton and tea. By 1960 almost half the country's cropland was controlled by these estates. The reduction in food crops led to frequent famines. Many farm workers fled to Tanzania where they joined the Frelimo independence movement.

When Mozambique became independent in the mid-1970s, Frelimo leaders tried to reform rural life by establishing large Soviet-style collective farms and state-owned farms. Although farm families now had a voice in farm management, most disliked the system and welcomed the return to traditional villages.

A rural Mozambican woman loads her laundry on the back of her bicycle. Transportation infrastructure in rural areas, especially in the north, is scant.

Family farms can produce some cash crops, such as cashew nuts, cotton, copra, and sisal.

REGIONAL VARIATIONS

Geography has had a strong influence on rural ways of living. The differences are especially marked between north and south.

Northern Mozambique has the most densely populated rural areas, including the provinces of Nampula, Niassa, and Cabo Delgado. The entire region is one of great scenic beauty. The coast has picturesque beaches and beautiful offshore islands. The interior coastal plain rises in the west to the cool breezes of the Lichinga Plateau and scenic Lake Malawi. Although the northern three provinces have nearly 40 percent of Mozambique's population, Niassa Province has the lowest density of any province. Historians have concluded that the small population is the result of three factors: years of slave raids that resulted in the enslavement of thousands of people every year; a long period of endemic sleeping sickness transmitted by tsetse flies; and infertile soil.

Ethnic traditions and location have made it difficult to introduce new ways of living or farming. The Makonde, for example, have always preferred their traditional patterns of subsistence farming. In addition, the north has been quite isolated from Maputo. North-south roads and railroads have been developed only in the past few years, and there were few radios until recently. New farming ideas and techniques could not be introduced in written form either, because fewer than 10 percent of the people could read or write.

Farming is more productive in central Mozambique, at least in the Zambezi Valley, and in coastal regions throughout southern Mozambique. Good soil and sufficient precipitation have contributed to more intensive vegetable farming. Fields of manioc (cassava) and corn provide two staples, while rice, sugar, tea, and citrus plantations provide important cash income.

Farm markets with abundant goods in Maputo, Beira, and other urban centers can create the impression that food production is not a problem in Mozambique. Inland from the coast and the river valleys, however, the climate is drier and the land less fertile. In large areas of Sofala, Manica, Tete, and Zambezia provinces, the land is hilly and dry, with baobab trees dotting the landscape. Farms here are spread out, and families struggle against drought, poverty, and disease.

Even in the poorest areas there has been a slow but steady improvement in the people's standard of living. The government has encouraged the creation of agricultural associations, allowing rural people to work together to improve conditions. "We formed our association four years ago," a woman explained to a UN worker. "The government has helped us with good seeds. We grow more food than ever before, and we sell rice, beer, and soft drinks in town. I don't know what happens in the future, but for now the association has been wonderful."

A local farmer loosens the soil with a hoe in a vegetable farm in a village in northern Mozambique. Agriculture is a dominant sector in the country's economy and the rural community depends on it for survival.

Opposite: **Snorkeling in Benguela Island in Bazaruto Archipelago off the coast of Mozambique. Such water activities help boost tourism in the country and provide jobs and revenue to the local population.**

Below: **Crowds of both locals and tourists at Costa do Sol in Maputo. Maputo's white sandy beaches and clear pristine waters provide respite from the urban rush.**

ISLAND AND COASTAL LIFESTYLES

The Indian Ocean coast and the dozens of offshore islands provide a totally different dimension of Mozambican ways of living. The most developed area in terms of tourism is Inhambane Province in the south. There are miles of sandy beaches dotted with palm trees. The calm, clear waters of the Indian Ocean invite a variety of water sports, including fishing, sailing, scuba diving, and snorkeling.

Along the country's coast several thousand Mozambicans work at beautiful resorts in a wide variety of jobs, from concierge services and

kitchen help to managerial positions. In addition, many live in old coastal or island villages such as the town of Inhambane. Like other coastal and island communities, Inhambane was a thriving town long before the Portuguese arrived. In the 10th century, Muslim dhows plied the coast, and, by the 17th century, it was a major port in the trade for slaves and gold from the interior. Today some villagers make a living offering tours of the many ancient buildings, including a Roman Catholic cathedral.

Another community with both historical and resort possibilities is Mozambique Island (Ilha de Mocambique). This northern island began as a boat-building center about 1,000 years ago and soon established trade ties with Persia, Arabia, and India. The fort of Sao Sebastiao served as the capital of Portuguese East Africa until the late 19th century when the capital was transferred to Maputo. The fort is still a major tourist attraction. It is the oldest European fort south of the Sahara, and tourism provides work for many of the 7,000 residents. The island was declared a UNESCO Cultural Heritage Site in 1991 because of its many beautiful buildings, many of which date to the 16th century. Most of the historic buildings are located in the northern part of the island while the majority of the residents live in reed houses in the south.

Mozambican school-girls.

EDUCATION

Education suffered a serious setback from the civil war, as did most areas of life in Mozambique. More than 5,700 schools were closed throughout the 1980s. By the mid-1990s less than 30 percent of the local population was literate.

The education record of Portugal's colonial government was a poor one. Since more than 95 percent were considered second-class citizens, schooling was ignored or even suppressed. As a result, only 10 percent of the people were literate in 1975 when Mozambique won its independence. The Frelimo government launched a literacy campaign for children and made education compulsory for ages 6 to 12. Government leaders also hoped that the collective farms would promote education and increase literacy.

The civil war ended the Frelimo campaign, and schools remained open only in towns that escaped the fighting. In the years since the conflict ended, Mozambique has renewed the ambitious literacy campaign. By 2005 the literacy rate had risen to about 50 percent. According to government figures, 99 percent of Mozambican children attended primary school in 2002, the most recent year for which figures are available, but only 13 percent of older children were enrolled in secondary schools.

There are only three institutions of higher education in the entire country. Their combined enrollment was 9,774 in 2004. The only institution offering advanced degrees is Eduardo Mondlane University in Maputo. Several international agencies, including UNESCO and Oxfam, a worldwide development and relief agency, are now providing supplies, prefabricated school buildings, and volunteer teachers.

Mozambican schoolgirls during a lesson in an open village classroom. With an increasing population of young Mozambicans, the availability of quality education and trained teaching personnel is of special concern.

RELIGION

IN A COUNTRY MADE UP of some 200 distinct ethnic groups and more than 30 languages, it is hardly surprising that religion in Mozambique is characterized by remarkable diversity. About half the people of Mozambique follow one of the many religions in the country. Traditional belief systems vary widely, although all are animist (believing that all inanimate objects possess a spirit).

In the eighth century A.D. Muslim traders brought Islam to the coastal regions and offshore islands, and today approximately 20 percent of the people in Mozambique are Muslim. Christianity was introduced by the Portuguese in the 16th century, and missionaries converted some societies or clans to the Roman Catholic faith. Protestant missionaries arrived in the late 19th century but they have been most active in the past 50 years.

Left: **A Neo-Evangelical ceremony in a village in Mozambique.**

Opposite: **A Catholic cathedral in the capital of Maputo. Mozambique has a sizeable Catholic population.**

SPIRITUAL HELPERS

In addition to healers (*curandeiros*), people in many ethnic groups also rely on individuals who seem able to help them in mystical ways. Some are called *profetas* (in Portuguese), or spirit mediums, and others are known as *feiticeiros* (in Portuguese)—witch doctors. The *profetas* might seek a solution to a problem, such as avenging a wrong done or avoiding an illness, by conjuring up the spirit of a deceased family member or an ancestor. In many traditional religions people believe that the spirits of the dead live on and can influence the daily affairs of the living.

The *fieticeiros* use a great variety of techniques, such as charms or casting spells, to help ethnic members. Whether the individual is seeking a job promotion or trying to win the affection of another or seeking revenge for a wrong done, the *feiticeiro* will intervene in the matter. Both *feticeiros* and *profetas* are constantly in demand.

Above: **Water baptism conducted on the beach of Maputo.**

Opposite: **Makonde carvings of family ancestral spirits.**

Estimates of the total number of Christians in Mozambique vary widely. Some surveys conclude that up to 20 to 30 percent of Mozambicans are Christian, with the community fairly evenly divided between Roman Catholics and Protestants. One reason for the variation in estimates is that evangelical Protestant churches have been very active in the past few years. They have apparently gained many new converts, especially among people under the age of 35, but no one is sure just how many.

TRADITIONAL RELIGIONS

While official figures indicate that 50 percent of the people follow a African traditional religion, the influence of those established beliefs may be even greater. Many Mozambicans who belong to a mosque or a Christian church mix elements of animism into their beliefs. For example, some people believe that the spirits of dead family members can influence their lives; this faith enables them to add traditional ceremonies or prayers to the Christian belief in an afterlife.

All traditional religions are animist—the belief that every living thing possesses a vital force. In some there is also the conviction that inanimate objects, such as trees, clouds, or lakes, also have spirits. Because these spirits can influence one's life, people take steps to please the spirits or to avoid angering them. The appeasement act might be a prayer, a ritual, a sacrifice, the carrying of a charm, or some other customary practice.

The practices of traditional religions, which have existed for several thousand years, vary considerably from society to society, but nearly all of these include some form of a healer. These faith healers are called *curandeiros* in Portuguese. Many combine ancient practices with modern Western medicine. A *curandeiro* might first treat a sick person with ancient herbal remedies combined with a healing ritual, and then dispense modern pharmaceuticals, such as pain relievers or an anti-inflamatory. In many rural areas this may be the only medical treatment available.

VARIETIES OF CHRISTIANITY

Throughout the colonial period Roman Catholic missionaries enjoyed a favored position. They were especially active where the majority of

A cathedral at Independence Square in Maputo.

Portuguese lived—in the south around Maputo and in the Zambezi Valley. Today most of Mozambique's Catholics still live in these two areas. Catholics have built elegant cathedrals in Maputo and Beira, as well as beautiful churches in several cities.

Many Protestant churches and splinter groups have been active since the late 1800s. The larger, well-established churches, such as Presbyterian, Seventh-Day Adventists, and Baptists, gained converts throughout the 20th century, especially in urban areas.

A number of small, little-known churches has multiplied in the past twenty or thirty years. Some of these churches are led by charismatic individuals who prove particularly popular with young people. Services may be simple, informal, and are likely to be held in someone's home or a community center. Other small Protestant groups have been built around international peace movements. These became especially popular during the civil war. According to government reports, some Protestant churches are growing at the rate of 20 percent a year.

ISLAM IN MOZAMBIQUE

In many communities on Africa's east coast, all activity comes to a stop five times a day for the conducting of Muslim prayers. Islam was founded early in the seventh century by the Arab prophet Muhammad. The religion spread rapidly, first through the area of the Mediterranean Sea, then eastward across Asia as far as modern-day Indonesia, and south along the African coast and islands. In Mozambique, most of the Muslim population is in the north and along the coast and offshore islands.

A Muslim Mozambican boy.

Islam today is one of the world's major religions. It is monotheistic, that is, based on a belief in one God, whom they call Allah. Muslims share some beliefs of both Judaism and Christianity, such as accepting Abraham and Moses as great prophets. Jesus is also regarded as a prophet, but Muhammad is regarded as the last and greatest of the prophets.

One important element of Islam is called the Five Pillars of Islam, or the five things that are to be followed by all of the faithful. The first pillar requires answering the five daily calls to prayer. Five times each day an official called a muezzin issues the call to prayer, usually from a tower called a minaret. Prayer takes place in a mosque, if one is available. If not, Muslims just kneel on small prayer rugs wherever they are, bending

THE HIDDEN JEWISH MINORITY

Five hundred years ago, the Roman Catholic Church and the rulers of Spain launched the Inquisition—a campaign to eliminate nonbelievers from Catholic countries, meaning Jews as well as others. This often-ruthless program, which sometimes included torture and execution, spilled over into Spain's close neighbor, Portugal. Many Portuguese Jews fled to Portugal's new territories in eastern Africa.

The Portuguese Jews established a small community on Mozambique Island and later in Maputo. The Jewish community grew during World War II (1939–45), when many European Jews frantically escaped from Nazi Germany's genocide against all Jews.

Throughout their history in Mozambique many Jews had to practice their religion secretly. Many sent their children to Christian schools. When the Frelimo government came to power in 1975, the Jewish synagogues were closed and the Jews became even more invisible. When religious freedom was established again in the early 1990s, the small Jewish minority was able to practice their faith more openly than it ever had in the past.

low in the direction of the holy city of Mecca. The second pillar is to observe the holy month of Ramadan. Throughout the month the faithful fast during daylight hours, then feast and pray after sunset. The third pillar is that Muslims must believe in Allah as the only God and Muhammad as the last prophet, Allah's messenger. The fourth pillar is to perform the hajj, or the pilgrimage to Mecca, at least once in a Muslim's lifetime if possible. The last of the five Pillars is alms giving. While Muslims in the coastal regions of Mozambique are devout, most do not follow the rules of Islam quite as strictly as do Muslims in other countries.

Mozambicans walk past an old and intricately designed mosque in an old district of Maputo.

LANGUAGE

ALTHOUGH MORE THAN 30 languages are spoken in Mozambique, along with many dialects, the great majority of the people speak and understand at least one of the eight major African languages. All of the country's languages belong to the large Bantu language family.

About 500 A.D. the many Bantu people began a great migration from their original homelands in north central Africa. Over several centuries they moved south and east. Their languages spread and became increasingly diverse, eventually creating several hundred distinct languages and related dialects.

Portuguese remains the official language of Mozambique. Only about one-quarter of the people speak Portuguese, however; knowledge of the language is limited to those who have had at least some schooling. The fact that Portuguese is far from universal creates serious problems, because it is the language of business, government, law, and higher education. Mozambicans who have not gone to school, including hundreds of thousands who grew up in refugee camps, have almost no opportunity to advance in those areas.

The government has been trying to upgrade education, including literacy in Portuguese, but the lack of funds has hampered the effort. There are not enough schools or trained teachers. International agencies provide some help, and many schools have started using split sessions, with half the children attending school in the morning, the other half in the afternoon.

Above: **Mozambicans bargaining and shopping for fresh produce at a busy street market in Maputo.**

Opposite: **A village girl taking time out to read.**

95

Mozambican teenagers walk out from a class-room after lessons. Portuguese is taught in many schools in Maputo and is the official language of administration in the country.

REGIONAL LINGUISTIC VARIATIONS

There is no dominant indigenous language, just as there is no dominant ethnic group. Instead, language use is spread geographically, generally corresponding to ethnic groupings.

The eight major Bantu languages can be divided into three major groups. The largest language group is made up of the Makua-Lomwe languages, spoken by more than 30 percent of the population, primarily in the north. The Makonde are Makua speakers, as are the neighboring Yao along the shores of Lake Malawi.

Central Mozambique, especially the Zambezi Valley, has been a meeting place of different groups for centuries, and this is reflected in the languages spoken. A variety of dialects of both the Tsonga and Shona language groups are spoken here, and there are small enclaves of Portuguese.

A NEW NATIONAL LANGUAGE?

Portuguese has been the official national language since colonial times, but many Mozambicans think it is time for a change. One candidate for a new national language for Mozambique is English. A Maputo businessman explains: "All of our neighbors except Angola are English-speakers. Many of our trade partners use English and so do the international agencies that are helping us build a healthy economy. It simply makes sense to change now."

Some people feel that an even better choice for a new national language would be Swahili (also called KiSwahili). The language is widely used as a second language in northern Mozambique, especially in the coastal and island regions. A Muslim woman who manages an island resort hotel states that "Swahili is close to being a lingua franca [universally used language] for much of Africa below the Sahara. Because it's a Bantu language, it is easy for most tribes in Mozambique to understand it." She also points out that tourists and traders from Tanzania and Kenya make use of it.

The argument is also offered that now is the time to change the national language because it would be at least as easy to teach English or Swahili to everyone as it would be to teach Portuguese to the 75 percent who do not speak it. So far the Mozambique government remains committed to a literacy program based on Portuguese. (*Above:* A Portuguese street sign in Beira points toward the location of the Municipal Council of Beira.)

South of the Zambezi, the majority of the people speak dialects of Tsonga languages, languages that are also spoken in South Africa. The Tsonga language is spoken not only by the Tsonga people but also by the Chopi near the coast. Smaller groups, living between the Zambezi and Save rivers speak the Shona language and related dialects. In the extreme south and near the Malawi border are groups who speak Nguni, a language they brought from South Africa when they fled the Zulu expansion of the 19th century.

PORTUGUESE PRONUNCIATION

Mozambicans speak Portuguese with more of a singsong lilt than Europeans do. When there is a double vowel, both are pronounced separately.

compreendo	compre-endo
cooperação	coo-operassao
c	*ss*
cc	*ks*
ch	*sh*
ou	*o* sound, as in "window"
s	*z* or *sh* (at end of syllable)
x	*sh* or *s*
z	soft *j*

SWAHILI PRONUNCIATION

The stress in almost all Swahili words falls on the second-to-last syllable. When two vowels are next to each other, each is pronounced separately. *Kawaida* (meaning "usual") is pronounced ka-wa-EE-da. The simplest rule is to pronounce vowels correctly:

a	as in "calm"
e	as in "may"
i	as the *e* in "me"
o	as in "go"
u	as the *o* in "to"

SILENT LANGUAGE

People communicate not only with words, but also with actions, facial expressions, and gestures. Anthropologist Edward T. Hall gave this kind of nonverbal communication a name in his book *The Silent Language*. Hall pointed out that silent language differs from culture to culture and that our failure to read these nonverbal signals can lead to misunderstanding.

Some international agencies offer guidelines for volunteers living and working in Mozambique. The following are some examples of local etiquette to be observed:

• Always accept gifts, no matter how poor the giver is; to refuse the gift might shame him or her.

- Mozambicans are sincere in their greetings; it is always best to greet or say good-bye when someone enters or leaves a room.
- Accept gifts with both hands; only small, insignificant items are received with one hand. So to do that with a more costly gift might be insulting.
- At meals in rural villages, if you eat everything that is served to you, your host will think you are still hungry and will want to serve you more; accept it when served; if you leave just a little food, you are saying that you are satisfied.
- Handshakes usually consist of three parts: first, the normal American-style handshake; this is followed by linking of bent fingers while touching the ends of upward-pointing thumbs, then a repeat of the standard handshake.

WORDS AND PHRASES

ENGLISH	PORTUGUESE	SWAHILI
Greetings/Hello	*Hola*	*Salama, Jambo*
Good-bye	*Até logo*	*Kwa heri*
What is your name?	*Como se chama?*	*Jina lako nani?*
		Unaitwa nani?
My name is	*Chamo-me*	*Jina languni*
Thank you	*Obrigado*	*Asante*
Please	*Se faz favor*	*Tafadhali*
	[or] *Por favor*	
Excuse me	*Disculpe*	*Samahani*
	[or] *Perdoe-me*	
church	*igreja*	*kanisa*
mosque	*mesquita*	*misikiti*
bank	*banco*	*benki*
river	*rio*	*mto*
market	*mercado*	*soko*

ARTS

THE PEOPLE OF MOZAMBIQUE seem to have an inherent need to express themselves in creative ways. Visitors notice this most in the country's music. City streets are filled with the sound of drums and guitars day and night, most of it coming from live performances. Music is nearly as common in rural areas, where songs and the rhythms of homemade instruments seem to be woven into the fabric of people's daily lives.

The creative drive is expressed in a variety of ways. Lively dance performances are nearly as widespread as instrumental and vocal music. Crafts represent another way to create. Several ethnic groups are known for their woodworking, including masks and sculptures. Others are skilled at different kinds of basketry and at creating batiks. In addition, a number of artists are internationally recognized for their oil paintings.

Left: **An array of hand-crafted sculptures and wood carvings, alongside paintings done in the style of famous artist Malagatana, are displayed on Costa do Sol Beach.**

Opposite: **Sculptures and intricately carved ornaments on sale along a road in Mozambique.**

Village children dance to the beat of a traditional drum.

Although there was not much literature during the colonial period, the beginnings of the independence movement inspired an entire generation of writers and poets. Since the 1960s, there has been a steady increase in the production of stories and poetry.

MUSIC

Traditional music is played throughout the country, but there is a good deal of regional variation in both the kinds of instruments and in the types of music played. In the north, for instance, the Makonde are known for their wind instruments called *lupembe*, usually made from animal horn, although sometimes from gourds or wood. In the south the *trimbila*, similar to a xylophone, is the favored instrument of the Chopi people.

In terms of types of music, probably the most popular music in urban areas is known as *marrabenta*. This is lively music, inspired by traditional rhythms, with an irresistible beat that often sounds like calypso, the music of the Caribbean.

Marrabenta emerged late in the colonial period. The Portuguese distrusted the folklike rhythms and tried to suppress it, but after independence it resurfaced as the country's favorite music. A band called Orchestra Marrabenta made recordings in the 1980s that spread the music's fame throughout Africa and then the world. *Marrabenta* has often accompanied performances of dancers from the National Company of Song and Dance. When Orchestra Marrabenta broke up in 1989, some of the band's members formed Ghorwane, which continued to perform in Maputo. By this time, the musical form was known throughout the world as "Mozambican."

Mozambican musicians performing at an outdoor grill at a club along the coast of Mozambique.

By the early 21st century new individual performers and groups have emerged. Chico Antonio's band, for example, plays melodies based on traditional rhythms, using a combination of bongo drums, flute, and bass, combined with the acoustic and electric guitar. Another new generation performer is Leman, a trumpet player and former member of Orchestra Marrabenta. Leman mixes traditional rhythms and melodies with various modern sounds.

In southern Mozambique, especially along the coast, the *trimbila* orchestras of the Chopi people provide a contrast to *marrabenta*. Performed in orchestras of 30 or more, *trimbila* concerts consist of complicated arrangements and dances. Live performances attract large crowds throughout Mozambique and in other countries.

A reggae band performs at a club in Maputo. Reggae music is another style adopted by Mozambican musicians.

DANCE

Mozambicans are known throughout Africa as outstanding dancers, both in nightclub acts and in traditional theater performances. As in so many elements of the country's life, there are differences between dancing styles of the north and south.

Perhaps the most famous dance style in the north is called *tufo*, first developed on Mozambique Island. *Tufo* is a rather slow-paced dance probably influenced by Arabic dances. Normally it is performed only by women, accompanied by special *tufo* drums. The dancers wear matching sarongs, called *capulanas*, and scarves, producing an elegant, fluid movement.

In the south, the Chopi people perform a faster-paced dance with the *trimbila* orchestras. The dance, called the *makwaela*, features a cappella singing and fast, intricate foot percussion.

Live dance performances are frequent throughout the country. The Casa de Cultura in Maputo, for example, is the home of the National Company of Song and Dance. Tickets to the performances are fairly expensive, but rehearsals are usually open to the public at no cost. At Quelimane in central Mozambique, a regional Casa de Cultura puts on performances by Montes Namuli, the traditional dance group of Zambezia Province.

MAPIKO: A RITUAL DANCE

A traditional dance called the *mapiko* probably originated several centuries ago as a ritual designed to ensure men's dominance over women. The male dancer wears a special mask, which is decorated with dyes, pictures, and hair. His clothing is made from five pieces of cloth that cover him completely except for his fingers and toes. The dancer represents the spirit of a deceased person, and the dance is designed or choreographed to frighten women and young children, convincing them that only the men of the village can protect them from the spirits of the dead. Despite uncertainty about its origins, the *mapiko* remains one of the best known of the country's dances.

Books for sale in Mozambique.

LITERATURE

During most of the colonial period few Mozambicans could read and write Portuguese, and there was no literature in the traditional languages. That began to change when Mozambique's independence movement began. Two of the most famous poets of this early independence movement were Rui de Noronha and Noemia de Sousa. Both poets focused on the themes of nationalist identity and solidarity.

Late in the 1940s José Craveirinha began writing about the suffering of the people under Portuguese rule and called for a popular uprising. His protests led to his arrest and imprisonment. Freed after independence, Craveirinha is today regarded as one of Mozambique's greatest writers. His work, including *Poem of a Future Citizen*, is well known throughout the world. Another nationalist writer, and a contemporary of Craveirinha—Luis Bernardo Honwana—was famous for his powerful short stories, including *We Killed Mangey Dog* and *Dina*.

During the struggle for independence, freedom fighters in the Frelimo movement began writing about their lives and encounters. They wrote stories and poetry about their forest camps, the frequent marches, the ambushes, and the gun battles. Marcelino dos Santos was probably the most famous of these "guerrilla poets."

After independence was achieved in 1975, writers and poets felt more literary freedom from government interference, although censorship was used by Frelimo during the conflict against the Renamo rebels.

New Mozambican writers emerged during the 1990s, including Mia Couto, whose works include *Voices Made Night* and *Tale of the Two Who Returned from the Dead*. Other famous writers of the period are Ungulani

Ba Ka Khosa, Lina Magaia, and Eduardo White. A more recent international sensation was Farida Karodlia's *A Shattering of Silence*, a tale of a young girl's journey through Mozambique after the death of her family.

ART

The most famous painter in Mozambique is Malangatana Goenha Valente. His powerful art details the sufferings of the people during the colonial period and the civil war years. Malangatana's paintings have been exhibited in galleries around the world.

Another well-known artist is Bertina Lopes. Her work emerges from her research into the themes, colors, and designs of ethnic art and crafts. Another artist, Roberto Chichorro, has gained fame for his paintings of childhood memories. Paintings and sculptures of all of the country's artists are frequently exhibited in the National Art Museum in Maputo.

A mural created by famous Mozambican artist Malangatana Goenha Valente.

CRAFTS

Perhaps the most famous creative works in Mozambique are the wood carvings. Beautiful sandalwood sculptures are made in the south, and ebony carvings are produced by Makonde carvers in the north. The late Alberto Chissano was the most famous sculptor, and his work received international acclaim.

The main center of Makonde wood carving is in Cabo Delgado Province, followed by Nampula. Most carvings depict traditional themes, but a number of artisans are experimenting with more modern styles. Nkatunga is one of the new generation of sculptors producing striking sculptures of rural life.

Woodcarving is a traditional craft in Mozambique.

BODY ART

An art form that is disappearing is the tattooing of women's faces (*above*), arms, and backs. The process begins in a girl's teens, when she receives several hundred tiny cuts in intricate geometric patterns. The cuts are then rubbed with herbs and charcoal, creating slightly raised scar tissue that is darker than the surrounding skin. The process is repeated every year so that the design became permanent.

Tattooing was once regarded as the height of feminine beauty, but the practice has been slowly dying out over the past thirty years. The Frelimo movement, with its emphasis on socialist equality, discouraged Mozambicans from tattooing.

The Makonde and several other groups also developed the practice of stretching a woman's lips by inserting larger and larger wooden plates, or plaques. Frelimo leaders discouraged the practice by publicizing the idea that this form of art was developed to make women appear unattractive to slave traders. Historians suggest, however, that the emerging women's rights movement is the major reason women are turning away from both tattooing and lip stretching.

Handmade ceramic ware on sale along the beach front in Mozambique.

Mozambique craft workers are also well known for their ceremonial wooden masks. The masks are popular among wealthy Europeans and Americans for wall hangings.

Basketry and woven mats are other examples of outstanding Mozambican crafts. Palma, located in the north near the Tanzania border, is the unofficial capital of basketry. Most of the crafts are made in outlying villages, then sold at the weekly market in town.

The Saturday morning craft market at Maputo, called the Mercado Artesanato, is another important center for the display and sale of Mozambique's crafts. In addition to wood carvings, baskets, and woven mats, there are beautiful batiks and jewelry items crafted from semiprecious stones like malachite. There are also larger items, such as reed chairs, cabinets, and bookshelves.

FROM GUNS TO SCULPTURES

In the late 1990s a Mozambique agency began a unique program to show the world that this southeast African nation has turned its back on war. Volunteers traveled from village to village, asking people to turn in their weapons in the cause of peace. The weapons turned in would be used to create sculptures dedicated to a nonviolent future. The villagers, in turn, would be compensated with goods or money.

Throughout Mozambique villagers responded with enthusiasm. They turned in tons of rifles, revolvers, automatic weapons, grenades, land mines, and ammunition clips. In 2003–04 four sculptors—Kester, Hilario Nhatugueja, Fiel dos Santos (*above*), and Adelino Serafim Mate—produced sculptures like the "Tree of Life" (*above*), made entirely of decommissioned weapons, with whimsical creatures (birds, animals, insects) frolicking about the tree.

The "Tree of Life" and an entire "Peace Garden" was on display in 2005–06 at the British Museum in London. The sculptures then went on tour to other countries, spreading Mozambique's message of peace and hope.

LEISURE

SINCE MOST MOZAMBICANS are engaged in subsistence agriculture, they have little time for the kind of leisure activities Americans enjoy. There are few personal computers, for example, and few television sets. (There are only five television sets for every 1,000 people in Mozambique; in the United States there are 880 televisions for every 1,000 people.) Quite a few Mozambicans own bicycles, but these bicycles provide an important means of transportation rather than recreation.

Although Mozambicans have little free time, they find ways to enjoy a variety of activities. Women sing as they work in the fields, and children manage to play games. More than half the people live near water, giving them the opportunity to swim or to fish (for pleasure as well as to add to the food supply). Even the poorest enjoy many family activities, including celebrating birthdays, weddings, and holidays.

For Mozambique's growing middle class, as well as for tourists and foreign aid workers, the country's recreation potential is remarkable. Wildlife areas, beautiful cities, coastal regions, and offshore islands offer a wide array of leisure opportunities.

COASTAL RECREATION

For anyone who has daydreamed about being in a tropical paradise—a place where gentle breezes whisper through palm trees that border white-sand beaches and crystal-clear waters sparkle in the sun—that picture postcard image is an accurate description of coastal Mozambique. The country measures some 1,100 miles (1,770 km) from north to south, but the many bays and inlets extend the actual coastline to 1,535 miles (2,470 km), plus the coastlines of dozens of offshore islands. Much of the coast is a tropical paradise in its own right.

Opposite: **Village children make their own toys with whatever materials they have or can find. This bright young Mozambican boy single-handedly made the metal frame of a toy car with wire and reuses cans for its wheels.**

While many islands and coastal areas are practically uninhabited, other areas are idyllic recreation areas, crowded with visitors on holidays and school vacations. A steadily growing number of Mozambicans enjoy these resorts along with more and more tourists from neighboring countries. Smaller numbers come from Europe, the Persian Gulf States, and India.

Some recreation areas offer special activity opportunities. Scuba diving enthusiasts, for example, flock to resorts such as Ponta d'Ouro, Inhaca Island, and Bazaruto—places where there is a great variety of marine life and coral reefs. Ponta d'Ouro is also one of the favorite destinations for those interested in surfing.

The Bazaruto Archipelago offers some of the most challenging game fishing in the world. Large black and striped marlins are a favored autumn catch, and it is not uncommon for a fish to weigh as much as 800 pounds (365 kg). Other game fish include tuna, sailfish, king and queen mackerel, giant barracuda, and several species of kingfish (including the mighty trevall).

Dolphin-watching tours draw people to several offshore islands. Even more popular are dhow safaris, available around the Bazaruto Archipelago and from Iho Island. Dhows are picturesque boats, each with a single tall mast and sail. They have been in use for several thousand years and are still a common sight on Africa's Nile River, the Suez Canal, and inland lakes, as well as the coastal waters. Traditional boats could sail only with the wind, but modern dhows are equipped with outboard motors. Families can take a dhow for a day of fishing or diving, and enjoy a picnic. More ambitious trips around the islands take from two to four days.

Two activities that draw surprising numbers are bird-watching and shell collecting. Birdwatchers come from as far away as Europe and North America for bird-watching safaris. All are invited to contribute to the Mozambique

Atlas Bird Project—an effort to catalog all of the country's birds, including some that are extremely rare, such as Eleanora's falcon and the stripe-breasted canary. Bird-watching centers include seaside regions such as Bazaruto Archipelago and inland areas such as Gorongosa National Park.

Experts say that Mozambique's coastal areas and islands constitute one of the best regions in the world for shell collecting. Almost every shell found in the Indian Ocean and as far away as the western Pacific washes up on the beaches of Mozambique. Shell collectors from all over the world come in search of rare, or even new, species.

A dolphin greets tourists in the waters off the coast of an off-shore island near Mozambique.

WILDLIFE SAFARIS

The key to future prosperity is how much success Mozambique will have in restoring, then expanding tourism. While considerable progress is being made in drawing people to coastal areas, it is just as important to bring visitors to the country's wildlife areas.

The wildlife reserves and national parks suffered tremendous damage during the fighting from 1977 to 1992. Thousands of the big animals that draw visitors, such as lions and elephants, disappeared. Some were killed in the fighting or by land mines, others were taken by poachers, and many simply migrated into safer areas, which usually turned out to be in a neighboring country.

Mozambique has a number of wildlife reserves and six national parks (with the addition of Quirimbas National Park, situated on a number of islands in Cabo Delgado Province). Very few have roads, lodges, and other facilities to serve tourists. Gorongosa National Park, once one of the great tourist destinations in Southern Africa, currently has only limited facilities for visitors. Two of the parks, Zinave and Banhine are closed. Bazaruto Archipelago National Marine Park is busy, but it is a marine reserve and the great need at the moment is in the inland wildlife areas. Of the wildlife reserves, only Niassa Reserve (at Lake Malawi) and Maputo Special Reserve can cater to the needs of visitors.

The Mozambique government and a number of international agencies are trying to build the kind of facilities that both Mozambicans and foreign tourists can enjoy. Several kinds of safaris are available, all involving cameras rather than the guns used in the old days of trophy hunters. Groups of varying sizes hire vehicles with drivers who also serve as guides and help with the preparation of meals. The journey can take a day or even up to two weeks (longer in Tanzania and Kenya). Meals and sleeping facilities are provided at lodges, although some people prefer to rough it by sleeping in tents and cooking over an open fire.

ENTERTAINMENT

Mozambique's attractive cities and large towns provide many ways to fill leisure time. People enjoy sitting at sidewalk cafés observing bustling street scenes. Street vendors and outdoor markets sell handmade baskets, weavings, batiks, and jewelry, as well as fresh fruits, vegetables, seafood, and household goods. An afternoon or weekend stroll takes people through tree-lined streets or "old towns," featuring 16th-century churches and the crumbling stone walls of ancient forts.

Locals and tourists enjoy an outdoor grill along Costa da Sol in Mozambique.

A Mozambican man wears a Makonde mask outside the Gallery of Makonde Arts at Nampula Province.

The larger cities are also busy at night. Restaurants provide some of the best cuisine in Africa, with Portuguese, African, and Indian influences. Nightclubs, discos, pubs, and clubs offer dancing and many kinds of music, including American jazz and blues. Maputo's popular street fair, called Feira Popular, features amusement-park rides, such as bumper cars, as well as dozens of bars and restaurants.

There is also more sophisticated entertainment, such as Maputo's Casa de Culture (House of Culture) which provides outstanding performances by the National Company of Song and Dance. The Teatro Avenida offers performances by local theater groups, usually in Portuguese. Movie houses show fairly recent American and European films in the original language with Portuguese subtitles.

Mozambicans and visitors to the country enjoy a surprising number of museums. Maputo has an excellent National Art Museum as well as a Natural History Museum and a Geology Museum that provide interesting information about the country. In addition, the Money Museum offers a history of currency, including early forms of barter.

In rural areas dance is the favorite form of entertainment, and every ethnic group has its own unique dance style. The Chopi people in the south continue to perform an ancient hunting dance. The performers wear lion skins and carry long spears and large oval shields. The music is similar to Caribbean calypso.

In north central Mozambique the Makua men perform a lively dance on stilts, making their way around a village to the great delight of their audience. The women of Mozambique Island also combine dance with athletic skill in a dance that includes jumping rope to a fast beat.

SPORTS

A growing number of Mozambicans, as well as foreigners in the country for extended stays, enjoy a variety of Western-style sports. Many hotels provide gymnasiums and swimming pools, available to city residents as well as hotel guests. Maputo has public tennis courts in the Botanical Garden, and there is a golf course just outside the city.

Mozambique is also well known for soccer (known as football outside the United States). Boys and girls throughout the country play whenever they can. Some villagers even use a homemade ball made of rags or animal bladders if a real ball is not available, and two or four sticks serve as goals. Beaches often serve as playing fields.

For people of all ages, soccer is by far the most popular sport, both among spectators and participants. Throughout the country, semiprofessional teams play matches before packed stadiums, including Machava Stadium in Maputo, which seats 60,000 spectators.

The Mozambique national team has performed well in international competition, especially after the fighting stopped in 1992. For many years the country was most famous for providing outstanding players to European teams, especially Portugal, but since independence most athletes choose to strive to improve Mozambique's standing in the soccer world. On several occasions Mozambique has represented the region in the African Nations Cup finals.

Mozambique's Maria Mutola became a national hero in 2000 when she won the gold medal in the 800-meter race at the Summer Olympic Games in Sydney, Australia.

FESTIVALS

RELIGION AND POLITICS have shaped Mozambique's festival days over the past half century. The movement for independence and the Frelimo government's attempts to establish a socialist society led to a decline in religious celebrations, both Roman Catholic and Muslim. Subsequently, after Frelimo's retreat from socialism with the 1990 constitution, the major religious holidays were restored.

Throughout the country ethnic groups and villages choose their own ways to celebrate public holidays. They also have their own traditional celebrations and festivities.

Opposite: **A young Mozambican woman with a clay-like mask of flour paste on her face carries a bowl of corn on her head in celebration of the season's harvest.**

NATIONAL HOLIDAYS

The year begins with New Year's Day, as it does for nearly every country. In the cities and towns, people celebrate New Year's Eve with dinners, dances, parties, and a midnight toast. January 1 is the actual holiday when schools, businesses, and offices are closed.

On February 3, Mozambique celebrates Heroes Day, followed by National Day (formerly Independence Day) on June 25, and Victory Day, September 7; all three celebrate the country's independence from Portugal in 1975. Armed Forces Day, September 25, is a commemoration of the army's role in winning independence and in achieving peace in 1992.

These patriotic holidays are marked by parades and political speeches. In the late 1970s these days were also occasions for rallies in support of the Marxist ideals of a society based on complete equality. Three other public holidays—Women's Day (April 7), Workers Day (May 1), and Family Day (December 25)—were also part of Frelimo's efforts to create greater equality. They continue to be celebrated but with far less fanfare than in the past.

Kinship ties and the birth of a newborn are embraced and cherished by Mozambicans, and festivities are always celebrated with family members.

Mozambican villagers attending a Catholic mass.

There are several other days that the government considers days of commemoration, but they are not official public holidays, meaning that schools, offices, and businesses can stay open. The Day of African Unity is celebrated in large areas of the continent on May 25, and the same is true of International Children's Day on June 1. Two other commemorative days—Resistance Day, June 16, and Assumption of Power by the Transition Government, September 20—celebrate Mozambique's independence. Resistance Day marks the first time Frelimo fighters took up arms against the Portuguese. The Assumption of Power celebrates the transition to full independence. In addition, each city has its own public holiday. Maputo's day is November 10.

CHRISTIAN HOLIDAYS

When the Frelimo government took office in 1975, the leaders hoped to follow the Communist ideal of creating a society with no separate social classes and with no religion. Churches, mosques, and Hindu temples were closed, but Frelimo could not make the ban on religion stick. By 1990 the new constitution gave everyone the right to worship. As a concession to Marxist ideals, the constitution also stated that everyone also had the right "not to worship," but the people paid little attention to that, and quickly returned to their traditional religious practices.

Mozambique's Christians have special celebrations on Christmas, December 25, and Good Friday and Easter. Because the dates for Good Friday and Easter are figured according to the phases of the moon (the lunar calendar), the dates for these two are different every year but are usually in March or April.

A Mozambican family spends some quality time together over a home-cooked meal. Both believers and non-believers in Mozambique prepare and share a special meal with loved ones on Christmas day.

On Christmas Eve and Christmas Day, Christians in Mozambique gather at churches all over the country for a time of worship and celebration.

Christmas festivals are a favorite with nearly every ethnic group because celebrating a birth is an important part of traditional celebrations. Good Friday and Easter also fit in well with traditional ceremonies based on the idea that the spirits of the dead can return to earth and influence people's lives. Not surprisingly, the celebration of these days often includes elements of traditional ceremonies. Both Good Friday and Easter are again public holidays, while Christmas Day technically is the public holiday of Family Day.

ISLAMIC FESTIVALS

Like many Christian holidays, Muslim festivals are also timed according to the lunar calendar. The most important holy period in the Muslim year is the month of Ramadan. During that period every adult Muslim fasts

Right: **Mozambican Muslims responding to the call to prayer in Beira.**

Opposite: **A Mozambican youth plays a lively and joyful tune on a handmade xylophone. Music and dance feature predominantly in coastal festive celebrations.**

from dawn until dark every day, following the practice established by the Prophet Muhammad. The believers can eat from sunset until almost dawn.

Ramadan ends with Eid el-Fitr, a two- or three-day festival during which Muslims gather with family and friends for feasting, praying, and exchanging of gifts. It is also customary to go to services in the mosque at the end of the month and also to give generously to the poor. The birthday of Muhammad, the founder of Islam, is also celebrated during Mawlid al-Nabi.

TRADITIONAL CELEBRATIONS

Many traditional ethnic and family ceremonies have been replaced by Christian or Muslim practices, but some festivals remain unchanged. Many have rituals revolving around spring planting or a good autumn harvest.

In one Makonde celebration several men would "casually" announce that they have to go away for a few days. While they are gone, villagers prepare for the harvest festival. Suspense builds until one night, when the moon is just right, masked dancers leap into the village, waving torches, chanting, and beating drums. The people rush to join them. Three days and nights of feasting, singing, and dancing follow. When the celebration is over, the missing men return, and the villagers pretend that the masked dancers had disappeared.

FOOD

BECAUSE OF ITS LOCATION on the southeast corner of Africa, Mozambique looks as if it might be isolated from the rest of the world. For the past thousand years and more however, Mozambique has been greatly influenced by other parts of the planet. This is clearly illustrated by the foods Mozambicans rely on.

The country's farm families grow very few of the grains that their ancestors grew. One exception is millet, a grain that is used primarily in making homemade beer. Most of Mozambique's major foods originated in other countries and were imported. Oranges and lemons, for example, were brought from the eastern Mediterranean by Arab traders as early as the ninth century. Some crops came from parts of Asia. A few examples of such crops are rice and sugarcane from Indonesia, tea from China, and mangoes and ginger from India. These foods probably arrived in Mozambique after 1100.

A number of important crops came from the Americas. These include two of the most important staples: corn and cassava. Peanuts, cashew nuts, and pineapple also came from the Americas.

RURAL STAPLES

Rice, corn, and cassava are the staples in the diet of rural Mozambicans. One or more of these is eaten every day, providing a low-cost dish that is filling. The addition of sauces, fruits, or peanuts adds to the nutritional value.

One popular dish, called *ncima* or *posho*, is made from cassava and corn. Women prepare this porridgelike dish by grinding corn and cassava together, using a wooden pestle and a large, deep wooden bowl. Some water and spinachlike cassava leaves are added; then it is cooked into a thick, pale yellow porridge.

Cassava, also called manioc, is a large root that is native to South America and brought to Mozambique by the Portuguese in the 16th century. Known to Americans as the main ingredient in tapioca, Mozambicans sometimes bake it like a sweet potato, slice it, and dry it in the sun, or mash it to form a porridge.

Opposite: **A young Mozambican boy sells homemade snacks in the city.**

127

The dish is served in calabashes (hollowed gourds). Roasted peanuts might be added for flavor, along with a weak wine, *utchema*, made of palm leaves. Small chunks of chicken or meat can also be mixed in.

Many rural families sometimes have chicken, and in the south beef is not uncommon. Both are likely to be served with *piri-piri*, a very spicy red-pepper sauce that Mozambique is famous for. Chicken is also served in a stew with peanuts and pumpkin leaves. Meat and chicken are important sources of protein, but both are expensive, especially beef, so they are served only as a special treat.

Young Mozambican children work at a fruit and beverage stall at a street market.

COASTAL VARIATIONS

On the islands and in coastal areas, the abundance of seafood provides a varied menu. Mozambique is famous for its prawns (*camarões*) and lobster (*lagosta*). These are valuable exports and are also widely used in domestic recipes.

One popular dish is *macaza*, made with shrimp, lobster, or prawns. The shellfish is put on bamboo skewers and grilled over an open fire. *Bacalhao* is a stew made of dried and salted fish mixed with vegetables. And *chocos* is squid cooked in its own ink. Seafood dishes often include coconut, peppers, onions, or special leaves for seasoning. A dish called *mu-kwane*, made of seafood mixed with coconut and cassava leaves, can also be found.

A Mozambican vegetable seller displaying her produce.

EATING OUT

Rural Mozambicans rarely eat in restaurants, but restaurant dining is popular in the cities. Maputo, Beira, and several larger towns offer a mixture of cuisines—African, Indian, and Portuguese.

Not surprisingly, Mozambique's restaurants are best known for their seafood, often made with a touch of *piri-piri*. Seafood and chicken are usually served with rice or French fries. Many dishes have a Portuguese influence, often cooked with wine or the fortified wine called port. There are also restaurants serving Indian, Chinese, Italian, and Malaysian food, and most cities will also have a pizza parlor.

There are numerous fast food places, especially in Maputo. Diners can find American-style hamburgers, Tex-Mex items like burritos or tacos, rolls, pastries, and even quiches.

Beverages include the usual assortment of American and European soft drinks. Tea is the most common drink around the country, and homemade beer is popular. A variety of fruit juices is also available everywhere, and bottled water is increasingly common. Although several plantations grow excellent coffee, it is found almost exclusively in restaurants, rather than in people's homes.

SOPA DE FEIJAO VERDE (GREEN BEAN SOUP)

Makes 8 servings.

1½ quarts water
2 teaspoons salt
½ teaspoon pepper
3 large potatoes, cut in chunks
2 medium tomatoes, cut in chunks
2 large onions
1 pound fresh green beans, cut lengthwise (French cut)

Bring the water to a boil in a large (3-quart) saucepan. Add salt, pepper, potatoes, tomatoes, and onions. Simmer for 20 minutes, or until the vegetables are nearly done. Use a food mill or sieve to puree the mixture. It should be a thin puree. Now add the string beans, and simmer for about 10 minutes until the beans are tender. Serve in bowls.

FRESH PINEAPPLE DESSERT

Makes 8 servings.

1 large ripe pineapple
$\frac{1}{2}$ cup sugar
$\frac{3}{4}$ cup Concord grape juice

Peel and core the pineapple, and cut it into slices. Sprinkle sugar on both sides. Place the pineapple slices in a 2-quart bowl (glass or chinaware). Add grape juice. Cover the bowl and place it in the refrigerator for 2 or 3 hours. Turn the pineapple slices every 20 or 30 minutes. Turn one more time before serving on dessert dishes. Serve with both forks and spoons.

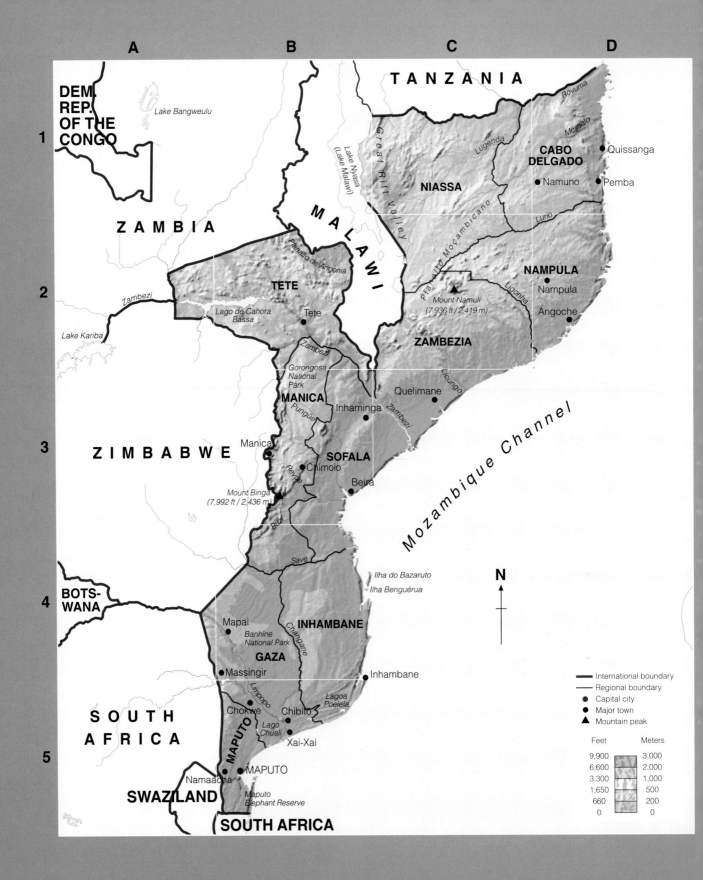

A | B | C | D

1

DEM. REP. OF THE CONGO

Lake Bangweulu

ZAMBIA

TANZANIA

Rovuma

Messalo

Lugenda

Great Rift Valley

NIASSA

Lake Nyasa (Lake Malawi)

M A L A W I

CABO DELGADO

Quissanga

Namuno

Pemba

Lurio

2

Planalto de Angonia

TETE

Zambezi

Lago de Cahora Bassa

Tete

Lake Kariba

Zambezi

Planalto Moçambicano

Mount Namuli (7,936 ft / 2,419 m)

ZAMBEZIA

Ligonha

NAMPULA

Nampula

Angoche

3

Gorongosa National Park

MANICA

Inhaminga

Pungüe

Quelimane

Licungo

Zambezi

Mozambique Channel

ZIMBABWE

Manica

Revue

Chimoio

SOFALA

Beira

Mount Binga (7,992 ft / 2,436 m)

Buzi

4

Save

Ilha do Bazaruto

Ilha Benguérua

N

BOTS-WANA

Mapai

Banhine National Park

Changane

INHAMBANE

GAZA

Massingir

Inhambane

5

Limpopo

Chokwe

Chibito

Lagoa Poelela

SOUTH AFRICA

Lago Chuali

Xai-Xai

MAPUTO

Namaacha

MAPUTO

SWAZILAND

Maputo Elephant Reserve

SOUTH AFRICA

International boundary

Regional boundary

● Capital city

● Major town

▲ Mountain peak

Feet		Meters
9,900		3,000
6,600		2,000
3,300		1,000
1,650		500
660		200
0		0

MAP OF MOZAMBIQUE

ECONOMIC MOZAMBIQUE

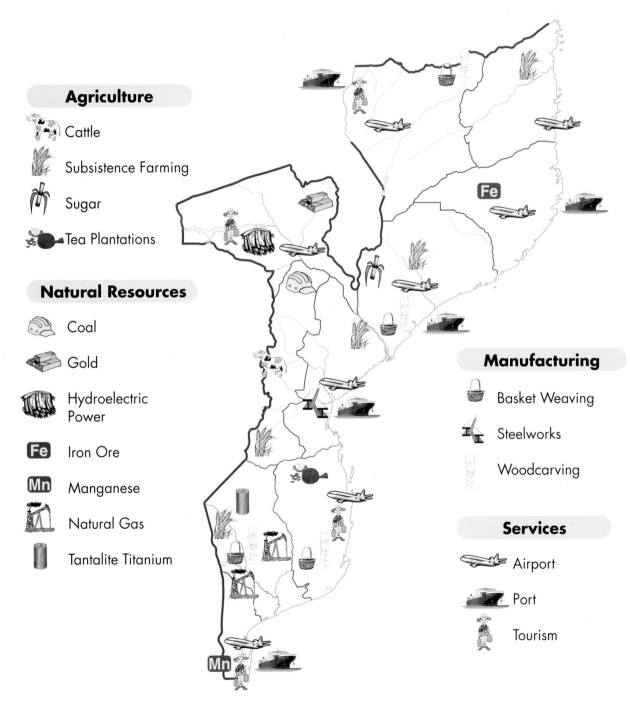

Agriculture

Cattle

Subsistence Farming

Sugar

Tea Plantations

Natural Resources

Coal

Gold

Hydroelectric Power

Fe   Iron Ore

Mn   Manganese

Natural Gas

Tantalite Titanium

Manufacturing

Basket Weaving

Steelworks

Woodcarving

Services

Airport

Port

Tourism

ABOUT THE ECONOMY

GROSS DOMESTIC PRODUCT (GDP)
$25.6 billion (2005 estimate)

GDP PER CAPITA
$1,300 (2005 estimate)

GDP GROWTH
7.0 percent (2005 estimate)

GDP SECTORS
Agriculture 24 percent, industry 41 percent, services 35 percent (2005 estimates)

LAND AREA
309,500 square miles (801,590 square km)

POPULATION
19,686,505 (July 2006)

UNEMPLOYMENT RATE
21 percent (1997 estimate)

POVERTY RATE
70 percent (2001 estimate)

CURRENCY
1 metical (MZM) = 100 centavos;
USD 1 = 26,500 Meticals (June 2006)

AGRICULTURAL PRODUCTS
Cotton, cashew nuts, sugar cane, tea, coconuts, cassava, corn, rice, bananas, pineapples, beef, poultry

MINERALS
Coal, titanium, natural gas, hydropower, graphite

INDUSTRIES
Food processing, beverages, chemicals, cement, petroleum products, textiles

MAJOR EXPORTS
Shellfish, cashew nuts, sugarcane, copra

MAJOR IMPORTS
Food, clothing, farm equipment, petroleum

MAJOR TRADING PARTNERS
South Africa, Portugal, United States, India, Australia, Zimbabwe

PORTS AND HARBORS
Maputo, Biera, Nacala, Inhambane

LEADING FOREIGN INVESTORS
South Africa, Portugal

INFLATION RATE
7.8 percent (2005 estimate)

CULTURAL MOZAMBIQUE

Mozambique Island
This island boasts historic architecture that includes Fort Sao Sebastion, this is where the oldest European fort in sub-Sahara Africa is situated.

Mercado Central Market
An outstanding open-air market that sells crafts, food, and household items.

Bazaruto Archipelago
Made a national park in 1971, the archipelago is a great destination for bird-watching, snorkeling, sighting whales or dolphins. Visitors may also tour marine safaris in motorized dhows.

1910 Railroad Station
This railway station features a dome designed by Gustave Eiffel.

Inhambane Province Coast
This long coast is the country's most highly developed area for tourism, with its outstanding beaches and wide array of water sports.

Ponta d'Ouro
A favorite tourist destination for visitors from South Africa, Ponta d'Ouro is known for its excellent beaches and is the prime area for fishing.

Maputo's "old town"
Home to outstanding historic architecture, including the Iron House.

Inhambane
Here stand many colonial-era buildings, including an 18th-century cathedral.

ABOUT THE CULTURE

OFFICIAL NAME
Republic of Mozambique

NATIONAL FLAG
The national flag consists of three horizontal bands: from top, green, white-edged black, and yellow. There is a red triangle on the hoist side, centered around a yellow star bearing an open white book on which are pictured a crossed rifle and a hoe in black. In 2005 a competition was announced to design a new flag and create a new national anthem.

NATIONAL ANTHEM
Patria Amada (*Beloved Motherland*)

CAPITAL
Maputo

OTHER MAJOR CITIES
Beira, Nampula, Chimoio, Xai-Xai, Inhambane, Quelimane, Angoche, Lumbo

POPULATION
19,686,505 (July 2006)

POPULATION DENSITY
63 per square mile (24 per square km)

LIFE EXPECTANCY
Approximately 39.82 years; men 39.53 years, women 40.13 years (2006 estimates)

ETHNIC GROUPS
Indigenous ethnic groups 99.6 percent

RELIGIOUS GROUPS
Indigenous belief systems 50 percent, Christian 20–30 percent, Muslim 15–20 percent

LANGUAGES
Portuguese (official), African languages, English

EDUCATION
Compulsory, ages 6–12

LITERACY RATE
47.8 percent (2003 estimate)

NATIONAL HOLIDAYS
New Year's Day (January 1), Heroes Day (February 3), Women's Day (April 7), Workers' Day (May 1), Independence Day (June 25), Armed Forces Day (September 25), Family Day (December 25)

FAMOUS MOZAMBICANS
Malangatana Goenha Valente, artist

TIME LINE

IN MOZAMBIQUE	IN THE WORLD
	753 B.C. Rome is founded.
	116–17 B.C. The Roman Empire reaches its greatest extent, under Emperor Trajan (98–17).
A.D. 100–300 Bantu societies migrate into the region and spread out.	
800–900 Arab traders establish posts on northern coast and islands.	**1000** The Chinese perfect gunpowder and begin to use it in warfare.
1498 Portuguese navigator Vasco da Gama stops at Mozambique Island en route to India.	
1507 Portuguese conquer Mozambique Island; it becomes the capital of Portuguese East Africa.	**1530** Beginning of trans-Atlantic slave trade organized by the Portuguese in Africa.
	1558–1603 Reign of Elizabeth I of England
Early 1600s The Dutch fail in their efforts to capture Mozambique Island.	**1620** Pilgrims sail the *Mayflower* to America.
1600s to 1800s Portuguese establish *prazeros* to control the people of the river valleys.	**1776** U.S. Declaration of Independence
	1789–99 The French Revolution
	1861 The U.S. Civil War begins.
1895 Colonial period starts.	**1869** The Suez Canal is opened.
1898 Lourenço Marques (later Maputo) becomes capital.	
1917 Portuguese put down Makonde rebellion in Zambezia Province, the last tribal uprising against Portugal.	**1914** World War I begins.
	1939 World War II begins.
	1945 The United States drops atomic bombs on Hiroshima and Nagasaki.
1950s Independence movement in Africa begins.	**1949** The North Atlantic Treaty Organization (NATO) is formed.

IN MOZAMBIQUE	IN THE WORLD
	1957 The Russians launch *Sputnik*.
1962 Front for the Liberation of Mozambique (Frelimo) is formed.	
1964–75 Frelimo wages revolution against Portuguese troops.	**1966–69** The Chinese Cultural Revolution
1969 Eduardo Mondlane is assassinated.	
1974 Mozambique is granted independence.	
1975 Frelimo gains control of government; Samora Machel is president.	
1977 Civil war pits Frelimo against the forces of Renamo (Mozambican National Resistance).	
1986 President Samora Machel is killed in a plane crash; Joaquim Chissano becomes president.	
1990 Frelimo government's new constitution ends experiment in communism.	**1991** Break-up of the Soviet Union
1992 The signing of the cease-fire treaty at the Rome Conference ends the civil war.	
1994 Joaquim Chissano is elected president in a free election. Renamo takes part and wins 112 seats in legislature.	
1995 Repatriation of civil war refugees is completed.	**1997** Hong Kong is returned to China.
1999 Joaquim Chissano is reelected for a 5-year term.	**2001** Terrorists crash planes in New York, Washington, D.C., and Pennsylvania.
	2003 War in Iraq
2004 Armando Guebuza is elected president, replacing Chissano.	

GLOSSARY

assimilados
African Mozambicans who could gain full rights of citizenship during colonial period only by meeting very strict requirements.

cassava
A thick root, also known as manioc or tapioca, that is one of the staples of the Mozambican diet.

copra
The white, meaty part of the coconut, used to make coconut oil, one of the country's major exports.

dhows
Sailboats with a single mast and sail that have been in use for several thousand years in coastal waters and on lakes and rivers.

Frelimo
Mozambique's liberation movement, which led the struggle for independence and remains the country's major political party.

indígenas
In Portugal's rigid class system, these were indigenous, or native-born Mozambicans, who had no citizenship rights.

mestiços
People of mixed Portuguese and African heritage.

matrilineal
The practice of tracing lineage through the mother, common in northern Mozambique.

patrilineal
Measuring descent and ancestry through the father, most common in southern Mozambique.

prazos
Large estates granted by the Portuguese colonial government to European landowners.

Renamo
Officially the Mozambican National Resistance, an opposition group that used guerilla tactics to launch Mozambique's costly civil war (1977–92). It has since become a political party.

shibalo
System of forced agricultural labor established by the Portuguese colonial government.

FURTHER INFORMATION

BOOKS

Hardy, Leanne. *The Wooden Ox*. Grand Rapids, MI: Kregel Publications, 2002.

James, R. S. *Major World Nations: Mozambique*. New York: Chelsea House Publishers, 1999.

Lauré, Jason and Ettagale Blauer. *Mozambique* (Enchantment of the World). Danbury, CT: Children's Press, 1995.

Mankell, Henning. *Secrets in the Fire*. Toronto: Annick Press, 2003.

Newlands, Glynne. *Mozambique: A Visual Souvenir*. London: New Holland Publishers, 2000.

WEB SITES

African News On-line, an excellent all-Africa site. www.africannews.org

Mozambique's embassy in the United States. www.embamoc-usa.org

Mozambique News Agency (English language). www.poptel.org.uk/mozambique-news

MUSIC

Complete listing of Mozambican CDs. www.mediaport.net/Music/Pays/mozambique/index.en.html

BIBLIOGRAPHY

Briggs, Philip and Velton, Ross. *Mozambique: The Bradt Travel Guide.* Guilford, CT: Globe Pequot Press, 2002.

Finnegan, William. *A Complicated War.* Berkeley: University of California Press, 1992.

Hanlon, Joseph. *Mozambique: Who Calls the Shots?* Oxford: James Currey Publisher, 1992.

Swaney, Deanna, et al. *Southern Africa.* Melbourne: Lonely Planet Publications, 2003.

Vine, Alex. *Renamo: From Terrorism to Democracy in Mozambique.* Oxford: James Currey Publisher, 1996.

INDEX